Conquering Your Past

Jeremy Lopez

Conquering Your Past

Published by Dr. Jeremy Lopez

Copyright © 2023

ENDORSEMENTS

Jeremy does an excellent job of giving balanced instruction on how to meditate, and also explaining the benefits that come from having a regular meditation and mindfulness practice. I love how Jeremy is not afraid to learn from and quote those outside the Christian tradition. He is able to explain the ancient concepts simply from a Biblical perspective. – Kari Browning, Director, *The Beautiful Revolution*

You are put on this earth with incredible potential and a divine destiny. This powerful, practical man shows you how to tap into power you did not even know you had. – Brian Tracy – Author, *The Power of Self Confidence*

I found myself savoring the concepts of the Law of Attraction merging with the Law of Creativity until slowly the beautiful truths seeped deeper into my thirsty soul. I am called to be a Creator! My friend, Dr. Jeremy Lopez, has a way of reminding us of our eternal 'I-Am-ness' while putting the tools in our hands to unlock our endless creative potential with the Divine mind. As a musical composer, I am excited to explore, with greater understanding, the infinite realm of possibilities as I place fingers on my piano and whisper, 'Let there be!' – Dony McGuire, Grammy Award winning artist and musical composer

Jeremy dives deep into the power of consciousness and shows us that we can create a world where the champion within us can shine and how we can manifest our desires to live a life of fulfillment. A must read! – Greg S. Reid – *Forbes* and *Inc.* top rated Keynote Speaker

I have been privileged to know Jeremy Lopez for many years, as well as sharing the platform with him at a number of conferences. Through this time, I have found him as a man of integrity, commitment, wisdom, and one of the most networked people I have met. Jeremy is an entrepreneur and a leader of leaders. He has amazing insights into leadership competencies and values. He has a passion to ignite this latent potential within individuals and organizations and provide ongoing development and coaching to bring about competitive advantage and success. I would highly recommend him as a speaker, coach, mentor, and consultant. – Chris Gaborit – Learning Leader, Trainer

Dr. Jeremy Lopez's book Universal Laws: Are They Biblical? is a breath of fresh air and much needed to answer the questions that people have been asking about the correlation between Biblical and Universal Laws. I have known Jeremy Lopez for years, and as a Biblical scholar, he gives an in-depth explanation and understanding of the perfect blending and merging into the secrets and mysteries of these miraculous Laws and how Bible-based the Universal Laws truly are. As the show host for the past twelve years on The Law of Attraction Radio Network, this book answers questions that I have received from Christian and spiritual seekers around the globe about the relationship between the metaphysical and Biblical truths. After reading this book, readers will feel empowered and have strong faith that God has indeed given us these Bible-based Universal and Divine Laws to tap into so that we can live and create an abundant life. – Constance Arnold, M.A., Author, Speaker, Professional Counselor, Host of *The Think, Believe & Manifest Talk Show*

TABLE OF CONTENTS

Preface	p.1
Introduction	p.21
"Chained"	p.41
The Meaning of Regret	p.71
Understanding Purpose	p.95
Letting Go	p.119
Moving On	p.139
Evaluating Ownership	p.165
Present Grace	p.183
Closing Thoughts	p.203

Preface

There was once a man named Benjamin. He was a quiet and introspective individual, known for his kind heart and gentle demeanor. However, there was a burden he carried with him—a deep-seated regret from his past that shadowed his every step.

In his youth, Benjamin had been brimming with ambition and dreams. He had aspired to become an artist, pouring his heart and soul into each stroke of the brush. But life had a way of intervening, and circumstances forced him to abandon his artistic pursuits. He had to put aside his dreams and take up a conventional job to support his family.

As the years rolled by, Benjamin's passion for art remained suppressed within him. He married, had children, and worked diligently to provide for his loved ones. But deep inside, a sense of longing and unfulfillment gnawed at his spirit. He often found himself gazing wistfully at the paintings and sculptures in galleries, imagining the life he could have led.

Regret settled in his heart like a heavy stone, weighing him down with each passing day. He became haunted by the "what ifs" and the missed opportunities. The vibrant colors of his youth faded into muted shades of remorse, casting a melancholic hue over his existence.

One day, while rummaging through the attic, Benjamin stumbled upon a dusty old canvas and a box of art supplies. Memories flooded back, and he was reminded of the artist he once aspired to be. His fingers traced the outlines of the forgotten brushes, now stiff and hardened with time. Something stirred within him—a flicker of hope amidst the sea of regret.

With a renewed sense of purpose, Benjamin decided to give his dreams another chance. Late into the night, he set up a makeshift studio in a corner of his basement, where he could paint undisturbed. Every evening, after his family had retired to bed, he would descend into the depths of his sanctuary and immerse himself in his art.

With each stroke, Benjamin found solace and a temporary reprieve from his regrets. The canvas became his confidant, absorbing his emotions and unspoken words. He poured his heart onto the blank surface, creating vivid landscapes, abstract masterpieces, and portraits that captured the essence of the human spirit.

Word of Benjamin's art slowly spread throughout the town. People marveled at the depth of emotion in his paintings, and galleries began to take notice. Yet, despite the recognition and praise, Benjamin's regrets persisted. He couldn't shake the feeling that he had wasted precious years and missed opportunities to truly explore his artistic potential.

One day, a young art enthusiast visited Benjamin's studio. She studied his paintings with awe, captivated by the raw emotions they evoked. Sensing the burden weighing on the artist's soul, she struck up a conversation with him. As they talked, she shared her own dreams of becoming an artist and the struggles she faced to pursue her passion.

Moved by her words, Benjamin realized that his regrets were not futile, but valuable lessons learned through hardship. He saw the chance to guide and encourage someone else not to make the same mistakes he had. He became a mentor to the young artist, providing guidance and support to help her navigate the treacherous path he had once walked.

Through mentoring, Benjamin discovered a newfound purpose—a way to make amends for the years he believed he had wasted. He realized that regret could be transformed into wisdom and compassion. As he watched his protégé blossom into a talented artist, he found redemption in his role as a teacher.

With time, Benjamin's regrets gradually lost their grip on him. He no longer saw his past as a series of missed opportunities, but as a stepping stone toward a greater understanding of himself and others. He began to see that life's twists and turns had shaped him into a compassionate and empathetic person—one who could offer guidance and support to those who needed it.

Benjamin's reputation as a mentor grew, and aspiring artists sought his wisdom from near and far. He opened his studio to young talents, hosting workshops and sharing his knowledge with unwavering enthusiasm. The once heavy burden of regret had transformed into a beacon of hope, illuminating the path for others to follow their dreams.

As the years passed, Benjamin's artwork continued to evolve, taking on new dimensions and exploring uncharted territories. He experimented with different styles and techniques, unafraid to push boundaries and challenge conventional norms. His paintings became vibrant expressions of his journey, reflecting not only the depths of his regrets but also the triumphs of his resilience.

The town celebrated Benjamin's artistic achievements, not just for the beauty of his creations but also for the profound impact he had on the community. Through his art and mentorship, he had inspired countless individuals to embrace their passions and live without regret.

Benjamin's story became a testament to the power of perseverance and the transformative nature of embracing one's true calling.

As Benjamin stood before a gallery showcasing his latest collection, he couldn't help but smile. The weight of regret had long been lifted from his shoulders, replaced by a sense of fulfillment and contentment. His journey had come full circle, from a man burdened by his past to a beacon of inspiration for others.

In that moment, Benjamin understood that regret was not a sentence to a lifetime of despair. It was an invitation to learn, grow, and redefine oneself. Through the darkness of his regrets, he had found a light—a light that now illuminated the path for others to find their own way.

And so, the man who once lived with regret became a symbol of hope, resilience, and the transformative power of embracing one's true passion. Benjamin's legacy lived on, not just in his artwork but in the lives he touched and the dreams he helped ignite. His story served as a reminder that it is never too late to pursue one's dreams and that even in the face of regret, redemption and purpose can be found. Often, we regret the things we failed to do as we ponder wasted time. Then, there are those things we regret actually doing.

We all make mistakes in life. At times, we may find ourselves haunted by the sins and transgressions of our past. Whether we have hurt others, made poor choices, or engaged in actions that we deeply regret, the weight of our past can weigh heavily on our souls. However, it is important to remember that the journey toward personal growth and transformation is not defined by our past mistakes, but rather by our ability to overcome them. In this chapter, we will explore the path of redemption and the steps we can take to rise above the sins of our past.

The first step toward overcoming the sins of your past is to confront them head-on. It is crucial to acknowledge the wrongs you have committed and take responsibility for your actions. Avoiding or denying the past only prolongs the pain and prevents true healing. By facing your past with honesty and courage, you open the door to self-forgiveness and the possibility of redemption.

Once you have confronted your past, it is essential to seek forgiveness from those you have wronged. Understand that forgiveness may not come easily or immediately. Some wounds take time to heal, and rebuilding trust can be a gradual process. However, by expressing genuine remorse, taking accountability, and making amends to the best of your ability, you create the opportunity for healing and reconciliation.

Every mistake we make in life provides an invaluable opportunity for growth and learning.

Reflect on the choices you made in the past and identify the underlying causes and patterns that led to those actions. By gaining a deeper understanding of yourself and your motivations, you can break free from negative cycles and make conscious choices aligned with your values. Embrace your mistakes as lessons and commit to personal growth moving forward.

Overcoming the sins of your past requires self-compassion. Recognize that you are human and fallible, just like everyone else. Beating yourself up over past mistakes serves no purpose and only hinders your progress. Treat yourself with kindness and understanding, acknowledging that you are on a journey of growth and transformation. Practice self-forgiveness and embrace the opportunity to become a better version of yourself.

Transformation is a continuous process. Embrace change and actively seek ways to improve yourself and your life. Surround yourself with positive influences, seek guidance from mentors or therapists, and engage in activities that promote personal development. By cultivating a growth mindset and staying committed to your own evolution, you can distance yourself from the sins of your past and create a brighter future.

One of the most powerful ways to overcome the sins of your past is to live authentically in the present. Embrace your newfound wisdom and use it to shape your actions and decisions. Align your life with your values and let go of behaviors that no longer serve you. By living in integrity and embracing a positive, purpose-driven life, you build a solid foundation for a future free from the shadows of your past.

Overcoming the sins of your past is a challenging but transformative journey. By confronting your mistakes, seeking forgiveness, learning from your past, practicing self-compassion, embracing change, and living authentically, you can rise above the burdens that have held you back. Remember, your past does not define you; it is merely a chapter in your life story. Embrace redemption, and let the lessons learned guide you toward a brighter and more fulfilling future.

As you navigate the path of overcoming the sins of your past, it is important to cultivate empathy and compassion not only for yourself but also for others. Recognize that everyone has their own struggles and imperfections, and they too may be grappling with their own past mistakes. By developing empathy, you can foster understanding and connect with others on a deeper level.

Empathy allows you to put yourself in someone else's shoes, to see the world from their perspective. This understanding can help you forge meaningful connections with others and facilitate healing. Through empathy, you can offer support and compassion to those who may have been affected by your past actions, demonstrating your genuine remorse and commitment to change.

Furthermore, practicing self-compassion goes hand in hand with empathy. Treat yourself with the same kindness and understanding you extend to others. Remember that you are on a journey of growth, and setbacks may occur along the way. Instead of dwelling on past mistakes, use them as fuel for personal transformation. Allow self-compassion to be your guiding light, reminding yourself that you deserve forgiveness and the chance to create a better future.

Overcoming the sins of your past requires a willingness to be vulnerable. It is through vulnerability that true healing and transformation can take place. Open up to trusted friends, family members, or professionals who can provide a safe space for you to share your story and express your emotions. By allowing yourself to be vulnerable, you invite others to offer their support, guidance, and wisdom.

Vulnerability also means acknowledging and addressing the root causes of your past sins. Dive deep into your own psyche, seeking to understand the underlying fears, insecurities, or traumas that may have contributed to your actions. By addressing these deeper wounds, you can take proactive steps toward healing and breaking free from destructive patterns.

Mindfulness is a powerful tool for overcoming the sins of your past. By living in the present moment and cultivating awareness, you can break free from the shackles of guilt and regret. Mindfulness allows you to observe your thoughts and emotions without judgment, creating space for self-reflection and acceptance.

In your journey toward redemption, forgiveness plays a pivotal role. Forgiving yourself and others is liberating and essential for healing. Remember that forgiveness does not mean condoning the actions or forgetting the impact they had. Rather, it is a conscious choice to let go of resentment, anger, and self-blame. Through forgiveness, you release the heavy burden of the past, opening yourself up to new possibilities and genuine transformation.

As you continue to overcome the sins of your past, embrace the power of gratitude. Focus on the blessings in your life and the lessons you have learned along the way. Gratitude fosters a positive mindset and helps you appreciate the present moment. By shifting your focus to gratitude, you can build resilience and find strength in the face of adversity.

Giving back to others is another powerful way to transcend your past and contribute to the greater good. Use your experiences and newfound wisdom to help others who may be facing similar challenges. By sharing your story, offering support, or engaging in acts of kindness, you create a ripple effect of positive change.

Overcoming the sins of your past requires courage, self-reflection, and a commitment to growth. By cultivating empathy and compassion, embracing vulnerability, practicing mindfulness and forgiveness, and nurturing gratitude while giving back, you can transform your life and leave the shadows of your past behind. Remember, redemption is possible, and every step you take toward healing brings you closer to a future filled with purpose, authenticity, and joy.

The weight of regret can be burdensome, dragging us down into a sea of "what ifs" and "if onlys." It's an emotion that grips us tightly, trapping us in the past and preventing us from moving forward. However, as we embark on a journey of self-discovery and personal growth, we must learn to overcome regret and embrace the power of letting go.

Regret is a natural human emotion. It stems from the realization that we made choices or took actions that led to negative outcomes or missed opportunities. Regret often arises from a sense of disappointment in ourselves and a longing for things to have been different. It's crucial to recognize that regret is a part of life and that everyone experiences it to some degree.

To overcome regret, we must start by accepting what has happened. Acknowledge the past and the choices made, understanding that dwelling on regret will not change what has already occurred. Instead, focus on cultivating self-compassion. Treat yourself with kindness and understanding, recognizing that you made the best decision you could at the time, given the circumstances and the information available.

Regret can be a powerful catalyst for growth. Use it as an opportunity to learn valuable lessons and gain insights into yourself. Reflect on the choices you made and the outcomes that followed. Ask yourself, "What can I learn from this experience?" and "How can I apply these lessons moving forward?" By reframing regret as a teacher, you can transform it into a source of wisdom and personal development.

Regret often blinds us to the positive aspects of our lives. Take a step back and challenge your negative thoughts. Instead of focusing on what went wrong, shift your perspective to the opportunities that lie ahead. Recognize that every experience, including the ones causing regret, contributes to your growth and resilience. By reframing regret as a stepping stone rather than an obstacle, you open yourself up to new possibilities.

Sometimes, regret stems from actions or words that have hurt others. In these cases, it's important to take responsibility for your actions and make amends where possible. Reach out to the people you have wronged, apologize sincerely, and seek forgiveness. Remember that healing is a process, and forgiveness may not always be granted. However, by taking these steps, you demonstrate your willingness to grow and repair the damage caused.

Regret keeps us trapped in the past, preventing us from fully experiencing the present moment. Embrace mindfulness and focus on the here and now. Practice gratitude for the opportunities and blessings in your life. By living in the present, you shift your attention away from regrets and start appreciating the beauty and potential that surround you.

The most effective way to overcome regret is to take action and make positive changes in your life. Identify the areas where you feel the most regret and explore how you can create new opportunities or make different choices moving forward. Channel your energy into pursuing your passions, setting goals, and taking steps toward a brighter future. Remember, it's never too late to start anew.

Overcoming regret can be a challenging process, and it's essential to seek support from those around you. Share your feelings with trusted friends or family members who can offer guidance and encouragement. Consider seeking professional help, such as therapy or counseling, to navigate the complex emotions associated with regret. Surrounding yourself with a supportive network can provide the strength and perspective needed to overcome regret.

Introduction

Regret is an ever-present companion in the journey of life. Each one of us has experienced those moments where we wish we could turn back time, undo our actions, or make different choices. It is a fundamental part of being human, for we are fallible creatures bound to make mistakes. In this chapter, we explore the reality that we all do things we regret, and how these experiences shape us.

Regret can manifest in various forms - from small, inconsequential decisions to monumental life-altering choices. It might be the words we spoke in haste, causing pain to a loved one, or the missed opportunities we failed to seize. It could be the chances we didn't take or the risks we were too afraid to embrace. Regret can also stem from the paths we chose that led us astray, or the dreams we abandoned in the pursuit of practicality. The scenarios are endless, but the feelings they evoke are universal.

What makes regret such a potent force in our lives is its ability to haunt us long after the moment has passed. We replay the scenes in our minds, dissecting the details, and wondering how things might have been different. It fills us with a sense of longing, an ache for the past that cannot be changed. We dwell on what could have been, tormenting ourselves with the burden of what we wish we had done differently.

Yet, within this darkness lies a glimmer of hope. Regret serves as a teacher, offering invaluable lessons that can shape our future actions. It reminds us of our fallibility, our capacity for growth, and the importance of making amends. Regret can be a catalyst for change, propelling us to become better versions of ourselves. It teaches us to value the present and make choices aligned with our deepest values.

To overcome regret, we must face it head-on. We must acknowledge our mistakes, accept responsibility for our actions, and strive to make things right. We cannot change the past, but we can learn from it. By taking ownership of our regrets, we empower ourselves to move forward with purpose and wisdom.

In this journey of self-reflection, it is crucial to practice self-compassion. We must recognize that we are all flawed and imperfect beings, prone to making errors. Beating ourselves up over past mistakes only perpetuates the cycle of regret and prevents us from healing. Instead, we should extend understanding and forgiveness to ourselves, allowing space for growth and transformation.

It is also important to remember that regrets do not define us. They are but fragments of our experiences, shaping us but not defining our entire being. Our lives are a tapestry woven with moments of joy, sorrow, triumph, and regret. Embracing this complexity allows us to find solace in the fact that regret, though painful, is an integral part of our human existence.

Ultimately, the key lies in moving forward. We must use our regrets as stepping stones toward a more fulfilling and purposeful life. We can make amends, seek forgiveness, and strive to create positive change. Each day presents an opportunity to make choices aligned with our values, to learn from the past, and to shape a future that embraces growth and resilience.

So, let us embrace our regrets as companions on our journey. Let us listen to their lessons, honor their presence, and use them as catalysts for personal transformation. In doing so, we may find that the weight of regret becomes lighter, and we can live our lives with greater authenticity, compassion, and purpose.

As we navigate the complexities of regret, we often find ourselves grappling with a range of emotions: guilt, shame, sorrow, and even anger. These emotions can be overwhelming, but it's essential to remember that they are a natural response to our actions and choices. Suppressing or ignoring these emotions only prolongs the healing process. Instead, we must confront them with honesty and vulnerability.

Sharing our regrets with trusted friends, family, or professionals can provide a sense of relief and perspective. It allows us to gain insights from others' experiences and receive the support we need to move forward. Opening up about our regrets requires courage, as it means exposing our vulnerabilities. However, it is through this vulnerability that we find connection and the understanding that we are not alone in our struggles.

In our quest to navigate regrets, it is crucial to cultivate self-forgiveness. Forgiving oneself is often one of the most challenging tasks we face. We tend to be our harshest critics, constantly replaying our mistakes in our minds and berating ourselves for the choices we made. But forgiveness is a powerful act of self-compassion and growth. It grants us permission to release the burden of our past, allowing us to live more fully in the present.

To forgive oneself, it is necessary to acknowledge the lessons learned from our regrets and use them as catalysts for personal growth. Reflecting on the experience and understanding what led to the regrettable actions or decisions can provide valuable insights into our thought patterns, values, and triggers. Armed with this self-awareness, we can consciously make different choices in the future and break free from the patterns that led to regret.

However, it is important to note that forgiveness does not mean forgetting or condoning our past mistakes. It means accepting that we are human and fallible, capable of change and redemption. Forgiveness is not a one-time event but an ongoing process. It requires patience, self-compassion, and a commitment to growth. Each day presents an opportunity to practice forgiveness, both toward ourselves and others.

Regret can also be a catalyst for repairing relationships and making amends. When our actions have caused harm to others, it is crucial to take responsibility, express genuine remorse, and seek reconciliation. While we cannot control how others respond or whether they choose to forgive us, making sincere efforts to make things right is an essential step in our personal healing and growth.

27

In some instances, regret may lead us to revisit past opportunities or dreams we let slip away. While we cannot turn back time, we can often find ways to pursue new paths or revive old aspirations. It might involve taking risks, stepping out of our comfort zones, or embracing opportunities that come our way. By doing so, we demonstrate our resilience and the capacity to create new beginnings, even in the face of regret.

Regret, when harnessed wisely, can be a catalyst for transformation and personal evolution. It compels us to examine our values, reassess our priorities, and strive for a life that aligns with our authentic selves. It teaches us the value of mindfulness, intentionality, and living with a sense of purpose.

So, as we continue our journey through life, let us remember that regret is an inevitable part of the human experience. It is through these moments of regret that we learn, grow, and ultimately become wiser, more compassionate beings. Embracing our regrets, acknowledging their lessons, and cultivating forgiveness within ourselves allows us to transcend the weight of regret and live with greater joy, fulfillment, and peace.

Regret has a way of shaping our perspectives and altering the course of our lives. It teaches us humility, reminding us that we are not infallible. Our regrets serve as reminders that we are constantly evolving, and with each regret, we have the opportunity to forge a new path.

One of the most significant challenges in dealing with regret is letting go of the past. We may become entangled in a web of "what ifs" and "should haves," which prevents us from fully embracing the present moment. The past cannot be changed, but we can change how we view it. Instead of dwelling on missed opportunities or wrong turns, we can shift our focus to the lessons learned and the growth that emerged from those experiences.

Regret also highlights the importance of living authentically. When we make decisions based on societal expectations or external pressures, we often find ourselves regretting those choices. Authentic living requires introspection, self-discovery, and the courage to follow our hearts and intuition. By aligning our actions with our true values and passions, we minimize the likelihood of future regrets and create a life that feels genuine and fulfilling.

While regret can be a powerful motivator for change, it's essential not to become consumed by it. Continually dwelling on past mistakes or allowing regret to define our identities can lead to self-sabotage and stagnation. It's crucial to strike a balance between learning from our regrets and letting go, allowing ourselves to move forward and embrace new possibilities.

Another aspect of regret is the role it plays in fostering empathy and compassion. When we reflect on our own regrets, we gain a deeper understanding of the challenges others may face. Our own experiences of regret can make us more empathetic toward the regrets of others, fostering connections and strengthening our capacity for forgiveness and understanding.

It's important to recognize that not all regrets are equal. Some regrets may be minor, fleeting moments of disappointment, while others may be deeply profound and life-altering. By distinguishing between the two, we can allocate our emotional energy more effectively. We can prioritize addressing the regrets that carry the most significant weight and work towards resolving them, while also learning to accept the smaller regrets as part of our human experience.

It is worth noting that regret is not a sign of failure but a testament to our growth and evolution. The fact that we can look back and recognize our missteps or missed opportunities demonstrates our capacity for self-reflection and personal development. Regret serves as a reminder that we are not stagnant beings, but ever-evolving individuals who have the power to learn, adapt, and make different choices in the future.

Regret is an integral part of the human experience. We all make mistakes and face moments of remorse. However, it is how we navigate and learn from these regrets that truly matters. By embracing self-forgiveness, pursuing authenticity, and cultivating empathy, we can transform regret into a catalyst for personal growth and positive change. It is through this process that we can release the weight of regret, freeing ourselves to live more purposefully and wholeheartedly in the present.

As we delve deeper into the realm of regret, we uncover its profound impact on our emotional well-being and mental state. Regret has the power to consume our thoughts, overshadowing moments of joy and hindering our ability to find peace within ourselves. It is crucial, therefore, to explore strategies for managing and overcoming the weight of regret.

One effective approach is practicing mindfulness. By cultivating present-moment awareness, we can redirect our attention away from past regrets and anchor ourselves in the here and now. Mindfulness allows us to observe our thoughts and emotions without judgment, creating space for acceptance and self-compassion. Through practices like meditation, deep breathing, or engaging in activities that bring us joy, we can gradually let go of the grip of regret and find solace in the present moment.

Seeking support from others can also be instrumental in navigating the burden of regret. Sharing our regrets with trusted friends, family, or support groups allows us to externalize our thoughts and emotions. By expressing our feelings and receiving empathy and understanding, we gain a fresh perspective and reassurance that we are not alone in our struggles. Supportive relationships can provide comfort, guidance, and encouragement as we work through our regrets and find ways to move forward.

In addition to seeking external support, self-reflection plays a vital role in understanding and addressing our regrets. Taking the time to reflect on the underlying reasons behind our actions and decisions can help us uncover patterns and triggers that lead to regret. Engaging in journaling, therapy, or personal introspection can provide valuable insights into our thought processes, values, and aspirations. Armed with this self-awareness, we can make conscious choices aligned with our authentic selves and minimize future regrets.

Another powerful tool for managing regret is practicing self-forgiveness. It is essential to acknowledge that we are human, prone to making mistakes, and deserving of compassion and understanding. Self-forgiveness is an act of kindness towards ourselves, allowing us to release the burden of guilt and shame that accompanies regret. Through self-forgiveness, we grant ourselves permission to heal, grow, and move forward with renewed purpose and self-acceptance.

Redirecting our energy towards positive actions is a transformative way to transcend the weight of regret. Instead of dwelling on past mistakes, we can channel our focus and energy into activities that align with our values and bring us a sense of fulfillment. By setting meaningful goals, pursuing personal growth, and making a positive impact on the world around us, we actively create a future that mitigates the influence of past regrets.

It is crucial to remember that regret is not an indication of failure or inadequacy. It is a testament to our humanity and the richness of our experiences. Each regret we encounter provides an opportunity for learning, growth, and resilience. By reframing our perspective on regret, we can view it as a catalyst for personal development rather than a source of despair. Embracing the lessons learned from our regrets empowers us to lead more authentic, intentional, and fulfilling lives.

Managing the weight of regret requires a combination of self-reflection, self-forgiveness, mindfulness, and support from others. By cultivating these practices, we can gradually release the grip of regret and find solace in the present moment. Through self-compassion and a commitment to personal growth, we can transform regret into a stepping stone towards a brighter future. It is within our power to rise above the weight of regret and live a life guided by wisdom, resilience, and a deep appreciation for the transformative power of our experiences.

In the journey of life, we often find ourselves burdened by past mistakes, failures, and regrets. The weight of these past experiences can hinder our progress and hinder us from fully embracing the present and future. However, the Bible provides guidance on how we can overcome these burdens and move forward with a renewed sense of purpose and hope. In this chapter, we will explore what the Bible teaches about forgetting those things which are behind and the transformative power it holds.

The Bible acknowledges that we are all prone to sin and make mistakes. However, it also emphasizes the importance of repentance and seeking forgiveness from God. In Isaiah 43:25, God says, "I, even I, am He who blots out your transgressions for My own sake; and I will not remember your sins." This verse reminds us that when we genuinely repent and turn to God, He forgives us completely and chooses not to remember our past wrongdoings. Therefore, dwelling on guilt and regret serves no purpose because God has already forgiven us.

One of the central themes of the Bible is God's grace and mercy towards humanity. In Ephesians 2:8-9, it is written, "For by grace you have been saved through faith, and that not of yourselves; it is the gift of God, not of works, lest anyone should boast." This passage highlights that our salvation is not based on our own merits or past deeds but on God's unmerited favor. When we truly grasp the depth of God's grace, we can release ourselves from the burden of past failures and move forward with confidence in His love and forgiveness.

The Bible encourages us to renew our minds and transform our thinking patterns. In Romans 12:2, it says, "Do not be conformed to this world, but be transformed by the renewing of your mind, that you may prove what is that good and acceptable and perfect will of God." To forget the things that are behind, we must actively engage in renewing our minds with the truth of God's Word. By focusing on God's promises, His faithfulness, and His plans for our lives, we can break free from negative thought patterns and embrace a hopeful future.

In Philippians 3:13-14, the apostle Paul writes, "Brethren, I do not count myself to have apprehended; but one thing I do, forgetting those things which are behind and reaching forward to those things which are ahead, I press toward the goal for the prize of the upward call of God in Christ Jesus." Here, Paul reminds us that the key to moving forward is to let go of the past and fix our eyes on the future that God has prepared for us. Our focus should be on growing in our relationship with Him, fulfilling our purpose, and striving towards the eternal prize.

The Bible teaches us that dwelling on past mistakes, regrets, and failures only serves to hinder our progress and rob us of the joy and freedom found in Christ. To forget those things which are behind, we must embrace God's forgiveness, rest in His grace, renew our minds with His truth, and fix our eyes on the future. By doing so, we can walk forward in faith, knowing that God has a greater plan for our lives and that He is always with us, guiding us every step of the way.

"Chained"

Regret, like a chain, has a peculiar way of keeping us imprisoned within the confines of our past. It is a formidable force that binds our minds and restrains our progress. Each link represents a missed opportunity, a mistake, or an unfulfilled aspiration. As we accumulate regrets, the weight of the chain grows heavier, hindering our ability to move forward and stifling our potential for growth and happiness.

The first link of regret is forged by the choices we didn't make. Those moments when we hesitated, doubted, or simply let fear dictate our actions. We ponder what could have been if we had taken that leap of faith, pursued our passions, or embraced change. These unfulfilled possibilities haunt us, their echoes reminding us of the roads not taken. The first link is a constant reminder of the opportunities we let slip away, and it fuels the regret that follows.

The second link is created by mistakes and missteps. We are imperfect beings, prone to errors and poor judgment. We make decisions that we later regret, hurting ourselves or others in the process. The weight of this link drags us down, replaying the scenes of our failures in a loop of self-condemnation. We question our abilities and dwell on our shortcomings, allowing these mistakes to define us and hold us captive.

The third link emerges from the choices we made that did not align with our true selves. Society, family, or even our own insecurities may have influenced us to conform, to settle for a life that doesn't reflect our authentic desires. The third link represents the compromise we made, sacrificing our dreams for the comfort of familiarity. It becomes a symbol of the opportunities we denied ourselves, locking us within the boundaries of an unfulfilling existence.

The chain of regret tightens around us, affecting our present and future. It clouds our judgment, taints our perspective, and drains our vitality. We find ourselves stuck in a cycle of longing for what could have been, replaying past scenarios in our minds, and feeling trapped by the choices we regret. We become prisoners of our own remorse, unable to break free from the self-imposed limitations.

To overcome the imprisoning nature of regret, we must first acknowledge its power over us. We need to confront the pain, the disappointment, and the sense of loss that regret brings. Denying or suppressing these emotions only strengthens the chain, reinforcing our captivity. By accepting our regrets and facing them head-on, we can begin the process of liberation.

Next, we must learn from our regrets. Each link of the chain holds valuable lessons if we are willing to explore them. Mistakes teach us resilience and wisdom, showing us alternative paths to success. Missed opportunities highlight the importance of seizing the moment and not letting fear hold us back. The compromises we made teach us the value of authenticity and the necessity of aligning our actions with our true selves.

Finally, we must forgive ourselves. Regret thrives on self-blame and guilt, consuming our energy and preventing us from embracing the present. Forgiveness is the key that unlocks the chains of regret, releasing us from the burden of the past. We must acknowledge that we are only human, fallible and prone to mistakes. By forgiving ourselves, we grant permission to let go and move forward.

Regret can be a powerful motivator if we harness its energy in a positive way. Rather than allowing it to chain us to the past, we can use it as a catalyst for growth and change. By acknowledging our regrets, learning from them, and forgiving ourselves, we can break free from the imprisoning chains and embark on a new journey of self-discovery, fulfillment, and joy. Remember, it is never too late to redefine our path and pursue a life free from regret. Here are a few practical steps to help you in your journey towards liberation:

Take the time to introspect and identify the specific regrets that weigh you down. Write them down, allowing yourself to acknowledge and confront them. This process will help you gain clarity and understand the reasons behind your regrets.

Instead of dwelling on the mistakes and missed opportunities, extract the lessons they offer. Look for the silver lining in each experience, no matter how challenging it may have been. Embrace the wisdom gained and carry it forward as a guiding light for future decisions.

Accept that the past cannot be changed. Recognize that dwelling on regrets only prolongs your captivity. Shift your focus to the present moment and the actions you can take now to shape a better future. Acceptance allows you to release the grip of regret and embrace new possibilities.

Take charge of your life by setting new goals and aspirations that align with your true desires. Use the lessons learned from your regrets to fuel your determination and drive for a brighter future. Create a vision for yourself and outline the steps needed to make it a reality.

Be gentle with yourself as you navigate the process of letting go. Understand that everyone makes mistakes and experiences regret. Treat yourself with kindness and compassion, knowing that growth comes from self-forgiveness. Release any self-blame or guilt, allowing yourself to heal and move forward.

If possible, take proactive steps to make amends for past regrets. Reach out to those you may have hurt or disappointed and express your remorse. While you can't change the past, sincere apologies and making things right can provide a sense of closure and promote healing for both parties involved.

Surround yourself with positivity and cultivate an optimistic outlook. Engage in activities that bring you joy, nurture your well-being, and foster personal growth. Practice gratitude for the present moment and focus on the opportunities that lie ahead, rather than dwelling on what cannot be changed.

Remember, breaking free from the imprisoning chains of regret is a gradual process. It requires patience, self-reflection, and a willingness to let go. By embracing the lessons learned, forgiving yourself, and embracing new possibilities, you can transform regret from a binding chain into a catalyst for personal growth and fulfillment. Your future is waiting—take that first step towards liberation today.

Don't hesitate to seek support from trusted friends, family members, or even professional counselors or therapists. Sharing your regrets and discussing your feelings with others can provide valuable perspectives, guidance, and emotional support. Surrounding yourself with a supportive network can help you navigate the complexities of letting go and moving forward.

Cultivate mindfulness in your daily life by staying present in the moment and observing your thoughts and emotions without judgment. Use meditation or mindfulness techniques to quiet your mind and gain clarity. Engage in self-reflection regularly to assess your progress, identify any recurring patterns or triggers, and make necessary adjustments to your mindset and behavior.

Regrets can often shape the stories we tell ourselves about our lives. Challenge and reframe the negative narratives associated with your regrets. Instead of viewing them as chains that hold you back, view them as stepping stones that have led you to where you are today. Focus on the strength and resilience you've developed through overcoming challenges and use them as fuel for personal growth.

In addition to forgiving yourself, consider extending forgiveness to others who may have contributed to your regrets. Holding onto resentment or anger towards others only perpetuates the cycle of imprisonment. Letting go of grudges and embracing forgiveness liberates not only yourself but also allows for healing and growth in relationships.

Break free from the shackles of regret by stepping out of your comfort zone and embracing new experiences. Use the lessons learned from your regrets to make informed decisions, but don't let fear of making mistakes hold you back. Taking calculated risks allows for personal growth, self-discovery, and the possibility of creating a future filled with fulfillment and happiness.

Define your values and align your actions with them. Live each day with intention, making choices that reflect your authentic self and contribute to your overall well-being. Set meaningful goals and work towards them diligently. When you live with purpose, regrets lose their grip, and you create a life that is driven by passion, fulfillment, and personal satisfaction.

Remember, the process of breaking free from the imprisoning chains of regret requires commitment, self-reflection, and a willingness to embrace change. By implementing these strategies and approaches, you can gradually release yourself from the grip of regret and unlock the door to a future filled with possibilities, growth, and self-fulfillment. Seize the opportunity to redefine your life, unleash your true potential, and embark on a journey towards a regret-free existence.

Be kind and compassionate towards yourself as you navigate the journey of releasing regret. Understand that you are human, and making mistakes is a natural part of life. Treat yourself with the same kindness and understanding you would offer to a close friend. Remind yourself that you deserve forgiveness and the chance to move forward.

Regret often stems from a desire for perfection and an unrealistic expectation of flawless decision-making. Embrace the understanding that perfection is unattainable, and it's through our imperfections that we learn, grow, and evolve. Allow yourself to make mistakes and see them as opportunities for growth rather than reasons for regret.

Regret keeps us trapped in the past, preventing us from fully experiencing and enjoying the present moment. Practice mindfulness and bring your attention to the here and now. Engage in activities that bring you joy, whether it's pursuing a hobby, spending time with loved ones, or simply appreciating the beauty around you. By immersing yourself in the present, you break free from the chains of regret that bind you to the past.

Gratitude has the power to shift your perspective and break the cycle of regret. Take time each day to acknowledge and appreciate the positive aspects of your life. Focus on the blessings, opportunities, and experiences that have brought you joy and growth. By cultivating gratitude, you shift your energy towards positivity and create a mindset that fosters contentment and fulfillment.

Regret can often create a limiting belief that the future will be a repetition of past mistakes. Challenge this belief and actively rewrite the narrative of your future. Visualize the life you desire, set ambitious yet realistic goals, and take intentional steps towards creating that future. By focusing on creating a new and positive narrative, you break free from the chains of regret and open yourself up to endless possibilities.

If there are unresolved issues or unfinished business related to your regrets, seek closure where possible. This may involve having honest conversations, making amends, or finding ways to heal emotional wounds. Closure can provide a sense of resolution and allow you to move forward with a lighter heart and a clearer mind.

Taking care of your physical, mental, and emotional well-being is crucial in releasing the chains of regret. Engage in activities that nurture your body, such as exercise, healthy eating, and sufficient rest. Prioritize self-reflection and engage in practices like journaling or therapy to process and release negative emotions. Make time for activities that bring you joy, relaxation, and rejuvenation. By investing in self-care, you strengthen your resilience and create a solid foundation for personal growth and liberation from regret.

Remember, the journey towards releasing regret is a deeply personal one. It requires patience, self-compassion, and a commitment to your own well-being. By incorporating these practices into your life, you can gradually break free from the imprisoning chains of regret and embrace a future that is filled with possibility, growth, and inner peace. It's never too late to redefine your path and create a life that is free from the shackles of regret.

The Apostle Paul, formerly known as Saul of Tarsus, had a past that starkly contrasted with his newfound life as one of the most influential figures in early Christianity. Before his encounter with Jesus Christ on the road to Damascus, Paul was a zealous persecutor of the followers of the Way.

In his early years, Paul was raised in the city of Tarsus, known for its vibrant intellectual and cultural atmosphere. He grew up in a devout Jewish family, immersed in the teachings of the Torah and trained as a Pharisee. Paul's fervor for his Jewish heritage and religious traditions burned brightly within him, shaping his worldview and actions.

Driven by his zeal, Paul actively sought to eliminate what he perceived as a threat to Judaism—the followers of Jesus, whom he saw as a blasphemous sect. He witnessed the stoning of the first Christian martyr, Stephen, and played a part in persecuting the early Christian community. Paul's name struck fear into the hearts of those who dared to proclaim Jesus as the Messiah.

However, everything changed one fateful day as Paul journeyed to Damascus with a mission to arrest and bring back any believers in Jesus. As he traveled, a blinding light from heaven suddenly surrounded him, and he fell to the ground. In that moment, he heard a voice saying, "Saul, Saul, why do you persecute me?" Trembling and astonished, Paul responded,

"Who are you, Lord?" And the voice replied, "I am Jesus, whom you are persecuting."

This encounter marked the beginning of a profound transformation in Paul's life. Blinded by the light, both physically and spiritually, he spent three days in darkness, wrestling with the magnitude of what had transpired. In those moments of solitude, Paul reflected on the life he had led, the violence he had perpetuated, and the teachings of Jesus that he had vehemently opposed.

Ananias, a disciple of Jesus, was sent to Paul by divine instruction to lay his hands upon him and restore his sight. As Paul's eyes were opened, he saw not only the physical light but also the spiritual illumination that Jesus had brought into his life. From that moment onward, Paul would dedicate his entire being to spreading the gospel, which he once sought to extinguish.

The transformation of Paul was not only internal but also external. His fervent zeal, once directed toward persecuting Christians, became an unwavering passion for sharing the message of Jesus Christ. Paul went from being an enemy of the faith to becoming one of its most devoted proponents. He traveled tirelessly, preaching and teaching the gospel, planting churches, and writing letters that would later form a significant part of the New Testament.

Paul's past served as a constant reminder of God's redemptive power and the transformative nature of His grace. The apostle himself acknowledged his former life, never shying away from his past or its implications. He wrote in his letter to the Galatians, "For you have heard of my previous way of life in Judaism, how intensely I persecuted the church of God and tried to destroy it. But when God, who set me apart from my mother's womb and called me by His grace, was pleased to reveal His Son in me, so that I might preach Him among the Gentiles..."

Indeed, Paul's life stands as a testament to the boundless mercy of God, who can transform even the most hardened hearts and use them for His divine purposes. The apostle's past, once marked by hatred and violence, became a testimony of God's love and forgiveness, and his teachings continue to inspire and guide believers to this day.

The apostle Paul's life serves as a remarkable example of the transformative power of God's grace. His past as a persecutor of the early Christian community stands as a stark contrast to his newfound life as an apostle and ambassador for Christ.

Paul's encounter with Jesus on the road to Damascus not only opened his physical eyes but also unveiled the truth that had been veiled from him for so long. It shattered his preconceived notions, challenged his beliefs, and humbled his heart. In that transformative moment, Paul experienced a radical conversion that redirected the trajectory of his life.

From that point forward, Paul's zeal was no longer directed towards persecuting the followers of Jesus but towards spreading the gospel. He underwent a rigorous period of introspection, study, and revelation, immersing himself in the Scriptures and communing with other apostles and early Christian leaders. Through this process, he gained a deep understanding of the teachings of Jesus and the implications of His life, death, and resurrection.

Paul's transformation was not without its challenges. His past as a persecutor caused many early Christians to question his sincerity and trustworthiness. Yet, through unwavering commitment, perseverance, and a genuine display of love and humility, Paul won the respect and acceptance of the early Christian community.

Throughout his ministry, Paul faced immense opposition, persecution, and personal hardships. He endured beatings, imprisonments, shipwrecks, and constant danger. Yet, through it all, he remained steadfast, unwavering in his dedication to Christ and the proclamation of the gospel.

Paul's past, far from being a hindrance, became a powerful testimony of God's transformative work in his life. His intimate knowledge of Jewish law and tradition allowed him to effectively communicate the message of salvation to both Jews and Gentiles. He was able to bridge the gap between the two worlds, offering a message of hope, reconciliation, and salvation through Jesus Christ.

The apostle Paul's life continues to inspire and challenge believers today. His example reminds us that no one is beyond the reach of God's grace. It teaches us the power of forgiveness, redemption, and the transformative work of the Holy Spirit in our lives.

The transformation of the apostle Paul from a persecutor to an apostle serves as a powerful testament to the life-changing power of encountering Jesus Christ. His past, once marked by violence and opposition, became a platform for spreading the gospel and impacting countless lives throughout history. Paul's story stands as an enduring reminder that no one is beyond God's grace and that true transformation is possible through faith in Christ.

In the annals of Christian history, the name of the Apostle Paul stands as a testament to the transformative power of God's grace. His life, once marked by zealous persecution of the early church, underwent a radical transformation on the road to Damascus. From that moment forward, Paul became a fervent follower of Christ, dedicated to spreading the gospel and sharing the boundless love and grace he had experienced.

Throughout his epistles, Paul often referred to himself as a prisoner of Christ, emphasizing his unwavering commitment and dedication to the cause of Christ. However, there is one instance in which he uniquely described himself as a prisoner of the grace of God. This unique expression can be found in the Book of Ephesians, a letter written by Paul to the church in Ephesus during his imprisonment in Rome.

In Ephesians 3:1, Paul begins by stating, "For this reason, I, Paul, the prisoner of Christ Jesus for the sake of you Gentiles." Here, Paul explicitly acknowledges his physical imprisonment in Rome. However, he goes on to expand on the nature of his captivity, describing himself as a prisoner of the grace of God.

To understand the significance of this statement, we must delve into the broader context of Paul's writings. Throughout his ministry, Paul was acutely aware of his own shortcomings and the magnitude of God's grace in his life. He understood that his transformation from a persecutor to an apostle was solely by the grace of God. In his letter to the Galatians, he wrote, "But by the grace of God, I am what I am" (1 Corinthians 15:10).

Paul recognized that God's grace was not merely an abstract concept but a tangible force that had apprehended him and brought him into a new life. It was this transformative grace that made him a prisoner—a captive bound by the overwhelming love and mercy of God. He realized that his life was no longer his own, but a vessel through which God's grace could flow to others.

As Paul penned the words of Ephesians, he was physically confined, unable to freely move and preach the gospel. However, his imprisonment did not dampen his zeal or diminish his sense of purpose. In fact, it was precisely within the confines of his prison cell that Paul grasped the profound truth of his captivity to God's grace.

Being a prisoner of the grace of God meant that Paul was completely dependent on the power and provision of God. It meant surrendering his own desires and ambitions to fulfill the divine purpose set before him. Paul found freedom in his imprisonment, not because of his physical circumstances, but because he understood that God's grace was sufficient to sustain and empower him in every situation.

Paul's description of himself as a prisoner of the grace of God serves as a reminder to all believers of the transformative nature of God's grace. It is a grace that not only forgives sins but also empowers and transforms lives. It is a grace that compels us to live selflessly and sacrificially, fully surrendered to the will of God.

Paul's proclamation of being a prisoner of the grace of God was a profound acknowledgment of his own dependence on God and a recognition of the all-encompassing power of God's grace. It serves as a reminder to us that, like Paul, we too are captives of grace—bound by love, transformed by mercy, and empowered to live lives that reflect the extravagant grace we have received. May we embrace this divine captivity and allow God's grace to work in and through us, leading us to a life of purpose and fulfillment in Christ.

As Paul continued his letter to the Ephesians, he expounded further on the concept of being a prisoner of the grace of God. In Ephesians 3:2-3, he writes, "Surely you have heard about the administration of God's grace that was given to me for you, that is, the mystery made known to me by revelation."

Here, Paul reveals that the grace of God was not only bestowed upon him individually but was entrusted to him as a stewardship for the benefit of the Ephesian believers and all those who would come to know Christ. He understood that he had been granted divine insight into the mysteries of the gospel, and it was his responsibility to share this revelation with others.

Paul's imprisonment did not hinder the administration of God's grace; rather, it became a platform through which the grace of God could be magnified. While physically confined, he continued to proclaim the good news, writing letters and encouraging believers in various cities. His incarceration became an opportunity for him to express his faith and dependence on God's grace in the face of adversity.

In Ephesians 3:7-8, Paul further emphasizes the significance of being a prisoner of the grace of God: "I became a servant of this gospel by the gift of God's grace given me through the working of his power. Although I am less than the least of all the Lord's people, this grace was given me: to preach to the Gentiles the boundless riches of Christ."

Paul humbly acknowledges that his calling and the ability to fulfill it were all due to the grace of God. He considered himself unworthy of such a privilege, recognizing that he had been the chief of sinners before his encounter with Christ. Yet, it was precisely because of his past that the grace of God shone even brighter. His testimony served as a powerful demonstration of the transformative power of grace.

Being a prisoner of the grace of God meant that Paul's life was completely surrendered to the service of Christ. His purpose was to preach the gospel and reveal the immeasurable riches of Christ to both Jews and Gentiles. He recognized that the grace he had received was not to be hoarded or kept to himself but to be shared freely with all.

Moreover, Paul's understanding of being a prisoner of the grace of God went beyond his own experience. In Ephesians 3:14-19, he offers a prayer for the Ephesian believers, expressing his desire for them to comprehend the vast dimensions of God's love and the fullness of His grace. He longed for them to be rooted and established in love, filled with the knowledge of Christ's surpassing love that surpasses human understanding.

In essence, being a prisoner of the grace of God was a profound realization for Paul—a recognition that his life was forever changed and directed by the unmerited favor of God. It was an acknowledgement that he was bound to the cause

69

of Christ, constrained by love, and motivated by a burning passion to make known the riches of God's grace to a broken and lost world.

Paul's proclamation of being a prisoner of the grace of God speaks to the transformative power of God's grace in his life and the lives of all believers. It was a declaration of his complete dependence on God, his commitment to sharing the gospel, and his recognition of the surpassing love and mercy that had apprehended him. May we, too, embrace this divine captivity, allowing God's grace to captivate our hearts and propel us into a life of purpose, service, and unyielding devotion to Christ. Rather than being chained to the regret of the past, it is possible to be chained to the grace and to the love of God.

The Meaning of Regret

Life is an extraordinary journey filled with moments of joy, sorrow, triumphs, and failures. Every experience we encounter, every person we meet, and every decision we make has the potential to teach us valuable lessons. From the grandest of adventures to the simplest of daily routines, life is always ready to impart its wisdom upon us. In this chapter, we will explore how life serves as a constant teacher, guiding us through the lessons we need to learn.

Life is in a perpetual state of flux, and change is its most fundamental characteristic. It teaches us to adapt, to let go of the familiar and embrace the unknown. Whether it's a career change, a relocation, or the end of a relationship, life reminds us that change is inevitable and provides us with an opportunity to grow and evolve.

Life often presents us with obstacles and hardships, testing our resilience and inner strength. These challenges, though difficult, offer us the chance to develop resilience, perseverance, and problem-solving skills. They teach us to confront adversity with courage and determination, ultimately leading to personal growth and self-discovery.

Interactions with others provide some of life's most profound lessons. Through relationships, we learn to understand and empathize with different perspectives, emotions, and experiences. Life teaches us the importance of compassion, kindness, and the power of human connection.

Life has a way of humbling us through failure. Whether it's a setback in our careers or a personal disappointment, failure teaches us resilience and the importance of learning from our mistakes. It reminds us that success often comes after multiple attempts and encourages us to persevere, reevaluate our strategies, and try again.

Life teaches us that perfection is an illusion. It shows us that flaws and imperfections are part of the human experience and should be embraced rather than feared. Life encourages us to accept ourselves and others as imperfect beings and to find beauty and strength in our unique qualities.

In our fast-paced and hectic lives, we often forget to live in the present. Life constantly reminds us of the importance of mindfulness and being fully present in each moment. It teaches us to savor the simple joys, to find gratitude in the ordinary, and to cherish the fleeting nature of time.

Our lives encourage us to engage in introspection and self-reflection. Life teaches us to pause, evaluate our choices, and learn from our experiences. Through self-reflection, we gain insight into our values, desires, and purpose, leading us towards a more fulfilling and authentic life.

Life rarely follows a linear path. Unexpected twists and turns force us to be adaptable and flexible. We learn to adjust our plans, shift our perspectives, and find new solutions. Life teaches us the art of embracing uncertainty and embracing the unknown with an open mind and a willingness to explore new possibilities.

Life is a constant reminder that everything is transient. It teaches us to let go of attachments, whether they are material possessions, relationships, or circumstances. By accepting the impermanence of life, we learn to appreciate the present, value what we have, and make the most of every fleeting moment.

Existence is an ongoing process of personal growth and self-improvement. It teaches us that growth doesn't have an endpoint but is a continuous journey. Each experience offers an opportunity for self-discovery, learning, and transformation.

Life urges us to embrace a growth mindset, to seek knowledge and expand our horizons. It encourages us to step outside of our comfort zones and take risks, knowing that the greatest lessons often lie beyond the boundaries of familiarity.

Life teaches us to listen to our inner voice and trust our instincts. It reminds us that our intuition is a powerful guiding force, helping us make decisions aligned with our values and desires. By honing our intuition, we gain the confidence to navigate life's complexities with clarity and purpose.

Life exposes us to diverse cultures, beliefs, and perspectives. It teaches us the value of inclusivity, tolerance, and acceptance. Through encounters with different people and ideas, we learn to challenge our preconceptions, broaden our worldview, and foster a sense of unity amidst our differences.

In many ways, life is a constant balancing act, urging us to prioritize and harmonize different aspects of our lives. It teaches us the importance of maintaining a healthy work-life balance, nurturing relationships, and taking care of our physical, mental, and emotional well-being. Life encourages us to seek equilibrium and avoid the pitfalls of excessive indulgence or neglect.

Life has its own timeline, often requiring us to practice patience. It teaches us that not everything happens according to our desired schedule. Through delays, setbacks, and waiting periods, we learn the art of patience and the wisdom of trusting in the right timing. Life reminds us that some things are worth waiting for and that patience can lead to greater rewards.

Life is often a series of trial and error. It teaches us that mistakes are not failures but opportunities for growth and learning. When we acknowledge our mistakes, take responsibility, and learn from them, we pave the way for personal development and progress. Life encourages us to embrace a growth mindset and see failures as stepping stones to success.

Life teaches us the transformative power of forgiveness, both towards others and ourselves. It shows us that holding onto grudges and resentment only weighs us down, hindering our personal growth and happiness. By practicing forgiveness, we release the burden of the past, heal our wounds, and create space for compassion and healing.

Life often reminds us that simplicity is a source of profound joy and contentment. It teaches us to appreciate the beauty in simplicity, to declutter our lives from unnecessary complexities, and to find joy in the little things. Life encourages us to prioritize experiences over possessions and to cultivate a sense of gratitude for the simple pleasures that surround us.

Life teaches us the power of vulnerability and authentic connection. It encourages us to open our hearts, express our emotions, and share our stories. Through vulnerability, we foster deeper connections with others, cultivate empathy, and create spaces for genuine intimacy. Life reminds us that it is in our vulnerability that we find strength and forge meaningful relationships.

Life is filled with uncertainty, and it is in this uncertainty that we find opportunities for growth and transformation. It teaches us to let go of our need for control, to embrace the unknown, and to trust in the unfolding of life's journey. By accepting uncertainty, we become more adaptable, resilient, and open to the infinite possibilities that life presents.

Life teaches us the profound impact of gratitude on our overall well-being. It reminds us to cultivate an attitude of gratitude, to appreciate the blessings and lessons that come our way. By practicing gratitude, we shift our focus from what is lacking to what is present, nurturing a sense of contentment and joy.

Life is like an eternal teacher, ceaselessly imparting valuable lessons to those willing to learn. It presents us with a myriad of experiences, challenges, and relationships that shape our understanding of the world and ourselves. Whether we are aware of it or not, life is constantly guiding us towards personal growth, wisdom, and self-discovery.

Each lesson life teaches us is unique, tailored to our individual circumstances and needs. It offers us opportunities to develop resilience, adaptability, empathy, and self-awareness. It challenges us to confront our fears, embrace change, and step into the unknown. Life nudges us towards introspection, encouraging us to reflect on our choices, beliefs, and values.

Through the ups and downs, triumphs and failures, life reminds us of the impermanence of everything. It teaches us to cherish the present moment, for it is all we truly have. Life demonstrates the transformative power of forgiveness, compassion, and gratitude, showing us that healing and growth can emerge from even the most challenging circumstances.

The lessons life imparts are not confined to classrooms or textbooks. They are woven into the fabric of our everyday experiences, waiting to be recognized and embraced. Life teaches us that growth is not a destination but a continuous journey, urging us to embrace a lifelong pursuit of knowledge, wisdom, and personal development.

To fully benefit from life's teachings, we must cultivate a mindset of openness, curiosity, and receptiveness. We must be willing to embrace discomfort, to question our assumptions, and to challenge our own limitations. Life's lessons are often disguised as trials, setbacks, or even missed opportunities. It is through these experiences that we gain resilience, strength, and a deeper understanding of ourselves.

As we navigate the intricate web of life, let us approach each day with a sense of wonder and gratitude. Let us recognize the lessons that present themselves, both in moments of joy and moments of pain. By embracing life as our eternal teacher, we unlock the profound wisdom it offers, empowering us to live with purpose, compassion, and authenticity.

In the grand symphony of existence, life's lessons are the gentle whispers that guide us towards our highest potential. Let us embrace them, cherish them, and allow them to shape us into the best version of ourselves. For life, with its unwavering commitment to teaching, is a remarkable gift that never ceases to inspire, enlighten, and transform.

In the tapestry of life, mistakes are inevitable threads that weave through our journey. They come in various forms, from minor missteps to grave errors, but they all offer valuable opportunities for growth and self-improvement. The ability to learn from our mistakes and harness the power of our past experiences is a transformative skill that can guide us towards becoming better versions of ourselves. In this chapter, we will explore the profound wisdom that can be gained from acknowledging our mistakes and leveraging our past to shape a brighter future.

Reflecting on our past mistakes is an essential step towards personal growth. By pausing to examine the choices we made and the outcomes they produced, we gain invaluable insights into ourselves and our decision-making processes. It is important to approach this reflection with a mindset of self-compassion and curiosity rather than self-condemnation. When we adopt a non-judgmental stance, we open ourselves up to profound self-discovery and transformation.

As we delve into our past, we begin to notice patterns that emerge from our mistakes. These patterns can be behavioral, emotional, or cognitive in nature. By identifying these recurring themes, we gain a deeper understanding of our tendencies, weaknesses, and blind spots. Moreover, recognizing the triggers that lead to our mistakes helps us develop strategies to navigate similar situations in the future. Through this self-awareness, we become equipped to break destructive cycles and make more informed choices.

Mistakes provide fertile ground for personal development and growth. Each misstep is an opportunity to enhance our skills, broaden our perspectives, and refine our character. By embracing our mistakes, we unlock our potential to develop resilience, adaptability, and humility. As we encounter setbacks and failures, we cultivate the determination to persist and the courage to try again. These qualities lay the foundation for achieving success and fulfillment in our endeavors.

Our mistakes not only teach us about ourselves but also deepen our understanding of others. When we recognize the fallibility of our own actions, it becomes easier to empathize with the mistakes and struggles of those around us. Our past mistakes serve as a reminder that everyone is on their own unique journey, and compassion becomes an intrinsic part of our interactions. By extending empathy to others, we foster meaningful connections and contribute to a more harmonious world.

The stories of individuals who have overcome adversity and turned their mistakes into stepping stones can be a profound source of inspiration. History is replete with examples of individuals who transformed their failures into catalysts for remarkable achievements. When we study their narratives, we realize that our past does not define us, but rather, it shapes our character and provides us with an opportunity to create a compelling future. These stories of resilience and triumph inspire us to persevere, to dream boldly, and to seize the transformative power of our own mistakes.

Our mistakes hold the potential to be catalysts for growth, wisdom, and self-improvement. By embracing them with an open heart and a reflective mind, we unlock the transformative power of our past. Through self-awareness, empathy, and determination, we learn to navigate life's challenges with grace and resilience. Our mistakes become not just reminders of our fallibility, but stepping stones towards becoming the best versions of ourselves. As we embark on this journey of self-discovery, let us embrace our mistakes, for they are the fertile soil from which our personal growth and fulfillment bloom.

Mistakes, when viewed from a different perspective, can teach us gratitude. They remind us of the lessons we have learned, the growth we have experienced, and the opportunities that have arisen from overcoming adversity. Gratitude allows us to shift our focus from dwelling on our mistakes to appreciating the wisdom gained from them. By cultivating gratitude, we foster a positive mindset that fuels our motivation and propels us forward on our journey of personal development.

Learning from our mistakes requires a willingness to adjust our approach. As we gain insights into our past actions, we can make conscious changes to our behaviors, attitudes, and beliefs. It might mean acquiring new skills, seeking guidance from mentors, or adopting different perspectives. By embracing a growth mindset, we recognize that mistakes are not setbacks but stepping stones towards refinement and improvement. Adjusting our approach allows us to move forward with renewed clarity and purpose.

The true value of learning from mistakes lies in our ability to apply those lessons to future challenges. Armed with the knowledge and wisdom gained from our past experiences, we become better equipped to navigate similar situations in the future. We develop the foresight to anticipate potential pitfalls, make more informed decisions, and take calculated risks. As we integrate these lessons into our lives, we transform our mistakes into powerful tools that guide us towards success and fulfillment.

In our quest to learn from our mistakes, it is crucial to embrace forgiveness and self-compassion. We are all fallible beings, and dwelling on past mistakes with guilt and self-blame only hinders our growth. Forgiving ourselves allows us to release the burden of regret and move forward with a lighter heart. Self-compassion provides the nurturing environment we need to learn and grow. By treating ourselves with kindness, we create the space for self-reflection and the courage to make positive changes.

When we openly acknowledge our mistakes and share our journey of growth, we inspire others to do the same. By demonstrating vulnerability and resilience, we create an atmosphere of authenticity and openness. Our willingness to learn from our mistakes becomes a powerful example for those around us. Through our stories, we encourage others to embrace their own imperfections, to persevere in the face of challenges, and to embrace the transformative power of their past.

Our mistakes hold tremendous potential for personal growth, resilience, and self-improvement. By reflecting on our past, identifying patterns, and applying the lessons learned, we pave the way for a brighter future. Embracing our mistakes and leveraging the power of our past allows us to cultivate self-awareness, empathy, and gratitude. It empowers us to adjust our approach, apply newfound wisdom to future challenges, and inspire those around us. Let us embrace our mistakes as stepping stones on the path of becoming the best versions of ourselves, for it is through them that we truly thrive and create a life of meaning and fulfillment.

Learning from our mistakes requires adopting a growth mindset—a belief that our abilities and intelligence can be developed through dedication and effort. With a growth mindset, we view mistakes as opportunities for learning and improvement, rather than as indicators of failure. This mindset enables us to approach challenges with resilience and a willingness to persevere. By embracing a growth mindset, we unlock our potential for continuous growth and development.

Mistakes serve as mirrors that reflect our strengths, weaknesses, and blind spots. By cultivating self-awareness, we gain a deeper understanding of our thought patterns, motivations, and behaviors that led to those mistakes. This self-reflection allows us to make conscious choices aligned with our values and aspirations. As we become more attuned to ourselves, we develop the ability to make proactive decisions that steer us towards a more fulfilling and purpose-driven life.

Mistakes often come with valuable feedback from others. Seeking feedback and listening to diverse perspectives can provide us with fresh insights and alternative viewpoints. Constructive feedback helps us identify areas for improvement and refine our approach. By embracing feedback with an open mind, we create opportunities for growth and collaboration. We learn to value the perspectives of others and recognize that collective wisdom can propel us forward on our journey of self-improvement.

Mistakes challenge our conventional notions of success and encourage us to redefine what it truly means to us. Rather than measuring success solely by external achievements or societal standards, we begin to place greater emphasis on personal growth, resilience, and fulfillment. Mistakes teach us that setbacks are not permanent roadblocks but temporary detours on our path to success. By embracing a broader definition of success, we can celebrate our progress, embrace our imperfections, and find joy in the journey itself.

Our past experiences, including our mistakes, are an integral part of who we are in the present moment. By integrating the lessons learned from our mistakes into our daily lives, we create a strong foundation for personal growth. We draw upon the wisdom gained to make informed decisions, navigate challenges, and cultivate healthy relationships. As we honor the past by incorporating its lessons into our present, we build a future that reflects our resilience, growth, and the wisdom gained from our mistakes.

Learning from our mistakes and leveraging the power of our past is a transformative journey that shapes us into better versions of ourselves. By embracing reflection, self-awareness, and growth mindset, we unlock the profound wisdom hidden within our mistakes. We cultivate resilience, empathy, and gratitude, which enable us to approach life's challenges with courage and grace. As we integrate the lessons learned from our mistakes, we redefine success on our terms and create a life of fulfillment and purpose. Let us embrace the transformative power of our mistakes, for they hold the key to our personal evolution and the realization of our fullest potential.

Understanding Purpose

Life is a complex tapestry of events, experiences, and interactions. Sometimes, it may seem that certain occurrences or circumstances are random or meaningless. However, when we step back and take a broader perspective, we can begin to see that everything in life serves a greater purpose. In this chapter, we will explore how even the smallest details and seemingly insignificant moments play a vital role in shaping our journey and contributing to the larger tapestry of existence.

To understand the greater purpose of everything in life, we must first recognize the interconnectedness of all things. Like a vast web, each thread is connected to another, forming a complex and intricate network. Just as every thread is essential for the stability of the web, every aspect of life has its place and significance.

Every experience we encounter, whether positive or negative, offers valuable lessons and insights. Even the most challenging moments can teach us resilience, strength, and empathy. These lessons prepare us for future situations and help us grow as individuals. Without the trials and tribulations, we would not have the opportunity to develop wisdom and understanding.

Our actions, no matter how small, have a ripple effect that extends far beyond what we can see. A smile shared with a stranger can brighten their day and inspire them to spread kindness to others. A single act of generosity can create a chain reaction of goodwill. Our words, gestures, and choices carry the power to influence others and shape the world around us. Each action contributes to the collective consciousness and has the potential to create positive change.

Individually, we are but a small piece of the vast puzzle that is life. However, each person plays a unique role in the collective journey of humanity. Whether we are artists, doctors, teachers, or parents, our contributions are like brushstrokes on a canvas, forming a collective masterpiece. Each person's talents, skills, and passions serve a purpose in the grand tapestry of life.

It is not just significant events or grand achievements that hold purpose. Even the seemingly mundane aspects of life have their place in the greater scheme of things. The daily routines, the ordinary moments, and the seemingly insignificant tasks are essential in creating stability, balance, and growth. The way we approach our work, relationships, and responsibilities can bring meaning and purpose to even the most routine aspects of life.

Life is often filled with uncertainty and adversity. However, these challenges serve a purpose in our personal growth and evolution. They push us beyond our comfort zones, forcing us to discover new strengths and capabilities. In times of hardship, we often learn valuable lessons, develop resilience, and gain a deeper understanding of ourselves and the world around us.

While it may be difficult to see the greater purpose in every moment, it is crucial to trust the process of life. The intricate web of interconnectedness weaves together each experience, choice, and interaction. Just as a puzzle cannot be complete without every piece, our lives are part of a larger tapestry that extends beyond our individual understanding. By embracing trust and surrendering to the flow of life, we open ourselves to discovering the profound purpose behind every aspect of our existence.

Life is not a series of random events but a carefully orchestrated symphony of experiences, opportunities, and connections. From the mundane to the extraordinary, every aspect serves a greater purpose in shaping our individual journeys and contributing to the collective growth of humanity. By recognizing the interconnectedness of all things and trusting in the process of life, we can uncover the profound wisdom and purpose that lies within us.

Synchronicity and serendipity often come into play when we least expect them, revealing the hidden threads that connect seemingly unrelated events. These meaningful coincidences guide us towards our purpose and open doors we never knew existed. Paying attention to the synchronicities that unfold in our lives allows us to tap into the greater tapestry of existence and align ourselves with the paths meant for us.

Life is a constant cycle of growth, change, and transformation. Impermanence is an essential aspect of existence, reminding us that everything has its time and place. Through the process of letting go, we learn to release attachments to outcomes, relationships, and material possessions. This act of surrender allows space for new opportunities, relationships, and experiences that align with our highest purpose.

Taking time for introspection and self-discovery is a powerful tool for uncovering the greater purpose of our lives. Through reflection, we gain insight into our values, passions, and unique gifts. By understanding ourselves on a deeper level, we can make conscious choices that align with our authentic selves and contribute positively to the world around us.

Challenges and setbacks are not meant to hinder our progress but rather to test our resilience and ignite our inner strength. They provide us with opportunities for growth, self-reflection, and personal transformation. The difficulties we face serve as catalysts for change, propelling us toward our purpose and allowing us to emerge stronger and more resilient than before.

The relationships we form throughout our lives have profound significance. Each connection, whether brief or enduring, serves a purpose in our personal and collective growth. We have the power to inspire, support, and uplift one another, creating a ripple effect that extends far beyond our immediate circles. Nurturing relationships fosters a sense of belonging and interconnectedness, reminding us that we are part of something greater than ourselves.

The grandeur of life's greater purpose does not solely rely on extraordinary accomplishments but also on the small acts of kindness and compassion we extend to others. Each person has the capacity to make a difference, no matter how seemingly insignificant their actions may appear. By extending love, empathy, and support to those in need, we contribute to the collective well-being and create a ripple effect that has the power to transform lives.

As we explore the concept of the greater purpose of everything in life, we come to realize that every moment, every experience, and every interaction holds profound meaning. From the lessons learned through challenges to the interconnected web of relationships and synchronicities, our lives are intricately woven into the tapestry of existence. By embracing trust, self-reflection, and the power of our choices, we can align ourselves with our purpose and make a positive impact on the world around us. Through this understanding, we can navigate life's journey with a sense of purpose, gratitude, and profound appreciation for the interconnectedness of all things.

Nature serves as a powerful reminder of the greater purpose that exists within every aspect of life. The cycles of the seasons, the harmony of ecosystems, and the interconnectedness of all living beings reflect the wisdom and intelligence embedded in the natural world. When we align ourselves with nature and its rhythms, we tap into a deeper sense of purpose and interconnectedness, fostering a harmonious relationship with the environment and all living creatures.

Often, we search for meaning and purpose in extraordinary moments or monumental achievements. However, true fulfillment and purpose can also be found in the simplest of things. Taking a walk in nature, savoring a cup of tea, or engaging in a meaningful conversation can bring deep satisfaction and a sense of purpose. Embracing the beauty of ordinary moments allows us to fully appreciate the present and find joy in the small things that make up the tapestry of life.

Beyond our individual lives, each person's actions, thoughts, and intentions contribute to the collective evolution of human consciousness. As we cultivate inner growth, expand our awareness, and embody compassion, we create a ripple effect that influences the world around us. By raising our own consciousness and inspiring others to do the same, we contribute to the greater awakening and transformation of humanity.

In our pursuit of goals and achievements, we often become fixated on reaching a specific destination or outcome. However, true purpose lies not only in the end result but also in the journey itself. Every step we take, every experience we encounter, and every lesson we learn shapes us and contributes to our personal growth. By embracing the process and finding meaning in every moment, we gain a deeper appreciation for the richness and purpose inherent in the entirety of our life's journey.

There are moments when life unfolds in unexpected ways, defying our plans and expectations. In these moments, it is essential to trust in divine timing and surrender to the greater wisdom of the universe. Sometimes, what may appear as delays or detours are actually guiding us toward a more fulfilling path or preparing us for greater opportunities. Trusting in the inherent order and timing of life allows us to release control and align ourselves with the grander purpose that unfolds before us.

The greater purpose of everything in life is a tapestry woven with interconnectedness, growth, and meaning. From the mundane to the extraordinary, from challenges to synchronicities, and from individual journeys to the collective evolution of consciousness, each thread plays a crucial role in the fabric of existence. By embracing trust, aligning with nature, finding meaning in the ordinary, and honoring the journey, we can live a life infused with purpose, gratitude, and profound awareness of our interconnectedness with all of creation. In doing so, we can contribute to the greater unfolding of humanity's collective purpose and create a more harmonious and meaningful world for ourselves and future generations.

Throughout history, humans have sought to understand the workings of the universe. From ancient civilizations to modern scientific discoveries, we have strived to unravel the mysteries that surround us. One of the fundamental questions that has intrigued philosophers, scientists, and thinkers alike is the nature of good and evil, and how they shape our lives.

At first glance, the existence of evil, suffering, and adversity in the world may seem contradictory to the concept of a benevolent universe. How can there be any good in the bad? However, a deeper exploration reveals that the universe operates in a delicate balance, where even the negative aspects serve a purpose in our growth and development.

To comprehend this intricate interplay, we must first understand that the universe is an interconnected web of energy, constantly in motion. It operates through the principle of duality, where opposites coexist and complement each other. Good and evil, light and darkness, joy and sorrow are not isolated concepts but rather interconnected facets of existence.

Adversity and suffering can be viewed as catalysts for personal growth and transformation.

Just as a seed requires darkness, pressure, and struggle to break through the soil and blossom into a beautiful flower, humans often need challenges to bring out their full potential. Difficult times force us to dig deep within ourselves, tap into our inner strength, and discover untapped resources we may have never realized we possessed.

Furthermore, it is through facing and overcoming adversity that we cultivate resilience, empathy, and wisdom. The experiences that shake us to our core often become turning points in our lives, propelling us on a path of self-discovery and personal evolution. In the face of suffering, we find an opportunity for growth, healing, and the deepening of our connection with others.

Moreover, the existence of evil and negativity acts as a contrast that highlights and enhances the goodness in the world. Just as the night sky allows us to appreciate the brilliance of the stars, the presence of darkness accentuates the beauty of light. Without the existence of pain and suffering, the joy and happiness we experience would lose their meaning and significance. Adversity and challenges make us value and cherish the moments of love, peace, and joy that we encounter along our journey.

Additionally, the collective experience of pain and suffering can unite humanity, fostering compassion, solidarity, and the desire for positive change. It is often during times of adversity that we witness incredible acts of kindness, selflessness, and heroism. The shared struggle brings people together, transcending differences and reminding us of our common humanity. The very existence of evil can ignite a flame of righteousness within individuals, motivating them to work towards creating a more just and compassionate world.

The universe operates on a grand scale, beyond our comprehension, and encompasses far more than our immediate experiences. While we may not always understand or appreciate the purpose behind every instance of suffering or evil, it is essential to trust in the intricate workings of the cosmos. In the grand tapestry of existence, even the darkest threads serve a purpose, contributing to the overall pattern of growth, learning, and the expansion of consciousness.

The universe operates in a delicate balance, where even the presence of evil and suffering serves a purpose in our lives. Adversity can act as a catalyst for personal growth and transformation, nurturing resilience, empathy, and wisdom within us. Furthermore, the existence of darkness allows us to appreciate and cherish the light and goodness in the world. Ultimately, by recognizing the interconnectedness of all aspects of existence, we can strive to find meaning and purpose in both the good and the bad, embracing the full spectrum of human experience.

While the concept of finding good in the midst of bad may be difficult to grasp in the face of immense suffering or tragedy, it is important to remember that our perspective is often limited to our individual experiences and immediate circumstances. The universe, with its vastness and complexity, operates on a much larger scale, with a broader tapestry of interconnected events and outcomes.

One aspect that illustrates the presence of good even in the darkest of times is the resilience and strength of the human spirit. Throughout history, we have witnessed individuals and communities rising above adversity, displaying remarkable courage, compassion, and perseverance. In times of crisis, the innate goodness within us shines through as we extend a helping hand to those in need, unite in solidarity, and work towards rebuilding and healing.

Moreover, it is often through the most challenging experiences that profound personal transformation occurs. Difficult times can lead to self-reflection, introspection, and a reevaluation of our priorities and values. When we are pushed to our limits, we have the opportunity to confront our fears, break free from self-imposed limitations, and discover a deeper sense of purpose and meaning in our lives. The lessons learned from these trials can shape our character, enhance our empathy, and ignite a passion for making a positive difference in the world.

In the grand scheme of the universe, the existence of evil and suffering can also be seen as essential components of the cosmic balance. The concept of free will allows for the possibility of both good and evil actions, granting individuals the freedom to choose their path. While this freedom can lead to negative consequences, it also opens the door for acts of kindness, compassion, and love. Without the existence of choice, our capacity for growth and the expression of our true nature would be severely limited.

Furthermore, the challenges we encounter in life often serve as catalysts for collective progress and societal change. Throughout history, transformative movements and revolutions have emerged from the depths of injustice and oppression. The fight against inequality, discrimination, and other forms of evil has sparked social movements, inspired activism, and led to significant advancements in human rights. The existence of evil prompts us to question the status quo, challenge injustice, and strive for a better world.

It is important to note that the presence of good in the bad does not justify or diminish the impact of suffering or evil. Pain and adversity are real and deeply felt experiences that can leave lasting scars. It is natural and necessary to acknowledge and address the pain, both individually and collectively. However, by recognizing the potential for growth, resilience, and positive change that can arise from these experiences, we can find a glimmer of hope even in the darkest of times.

The universe operates in a delicate balance, where the presence of evil and suffering serves a purpose that extends beyond our immediate understanding. Through personal transformation, the resilience of the human spirit, and collective progress, we can discover the seeds of goodness in the midst of adversity. By embracing the interconnected nature of the universe and maintaining faith in the inherent capacity for growth and positive change, we can navigate the complexities of life with courage, compassion, and a commitment to creating a brighter future.

In times of hardship and adversity, it is natural for us to question why certain things happen and how they can possibly work for our good. The Bible provides us with profound wisdom and guidance in understanding that all things, even the most challenging ones, can ultimately be used for our benefit. This chapter will explore the biblical teachings that reassure us of God's sovereign plan and His ability to turn every circumstance to our advantage.

The Bible repeatedly emphasizes that God is in control of all things, and His plans are perfect. Despite our limited understanding, God sees the bigger picture and orchestrates everything according to His purpose.

Romans 8:28 (NIV) states, "And we know that in all things God works for the good of those who love him, who have been called according to his purpose." This verse assures us that God is actively working for our good, even in the midst of difficult situations.

Adversity often serves as a catalyst for personal growth and spiritual maturity. The Bible teaches us that trials can refine our character, deepen our faith, and produce perseverance.

James 1:2-4 (NIV) says, "Consider it pure joy, my brothers and sisters, whenever you face trials of many kinds because you know that the testing of your faith produces perseverance. Let perseverance finish its work so that you may be mature and complete, not lacking anything." This passage encourages us to view trials as an opportunity for growth, knowing that they ultimately contribute to our development as individuals.

The Bible teaches us to place our trust in God's provision and to have faith that He will work all things for our good. It reminds us that God is our loving Father, who cares for us deeply and meets our needs.

Philippians 4:19 (NIV) declares, "And my God will meet all your needs according to the riches of his glory in Christ Jesus." This verse reassures us that God is aware of our needs and will provide for us abundantly.

The Bible also instructs us to respond to adversity with love, forgiveness, and compassion. It teaches that by doing so, we can overcome evil and bring about positive change in our lives and the lives of others.

Romans 12:21 (NIV) encourages us, saying, "Do not be overcome by evil, but overcome evil with good." This verse reminds us that our actions have the power to transform difficult situations, as we choose to respond with kindness and seek reconciliation.

The Bible offers a profound perspective on how all things can work for our good. It teaches us to trust in God's sovereign plan, to embrace trials as opportunities for growth, to rely on His provision, and to respond to adversity with love and goodness. By studying and applying these biblical teachings, we can find comfort and hope in the midst of challenges, knowing that God is actively working for our ultimate good.

Letting Go

In life, we often accumulate various things—physical possessions, relationships, beliefs, and habits—that once served us well but now hinder our growth and happiness. These attachments can weigh us down, preventing us from moving forward and embracing new opportunities. In this chapter, we will explore the art of letting go, understanding why it is essential, and discovering practical strategies to release the things that no longer serve us. By cultivating the ability to let go, we open ourselves up to new possibilities and create space for growth and transformation.

The first step in letting go is recognizing the areas of our lives where things no longer serve us. Take a moment to reflect on your physical belongings, relationships, thought patterns, and behaviors. Ask yourself if they contribute positively to your life or if they hold you back. Consider the emotional, mental, and physical toll they might be taking. By acknowledging what no longer serves us, we empower ourselves to make conscious choices about what we want to release.

One of the fundamental truths of life is impermanence. Everything is constantly changing, and clinging to the past or resisting change only causes suffering. Embracing the impermanence of things can help us let go more gracefully. Remember that it is natural for people, circumstances, and even our own preferences to evolve over time. By accepting this truth, we free ourselves from the attachment to what was and open up to what can be.

Mindfulness is a powerful tool for letting go. By practicing present-moment awareness, we develop the ability to observe our thoughts, emotions, and attachments without judgment. Mindfulness allows us to recognize when we are holding onto something that no longer serves us and gives us the space to choose a different path. Through practices like meditation, deep breathing, and self-reflection, we can cultivate mindfulness and develop a greater sense of clarity and detachment.

Physical clutter can have a significant impact on our well-being and energy levels. Take a look at your living space and identify items that you no longer need, use, or truly value. Decluttering your physical environment can be liberating and create a sense of lightness. Consider donating or selling these items, allowing someone else to benefit from them. By letting go of the excess, you create room for new experiences and invite positive energy into your life.

Just as physical possessions can weigh us down, so too can toxic or unfulfilling relationships. Assess your relationships and identify any that no longer serve your well-being or align with your values. It may be challenging to let go of certain connections but remember that healthy relationships should uplift and support you. Surround yourself with people who encourage your growth and share your vision for a positive future. Release relationships that drain your energy and make space for healthier, more nourishing connections.

Our beliefs shape our reality. If we hold onto limiting beliefs that no longer serve us, they can hinder our personal and professional growth. Take a close look at the beliefs that are holding you back, such as "I'm not good enough," "I can't change," or "I don't deserve happiness." Challenge these beliefs by seeking evidence to the contrary and replacing them with empowering, positive affirmations. Let go of beliefs that no longer serve your highest good and embrace a mindset that supports your goals and aspirations.

Habits are deeply ingrained patterns of behavior that can either propel us forward or hold us back. Identify habits that no longer align with your desired outcomes and begin cultivating new habits that support your growth and well-being. Start by setting clear intentions for the habits you want to develop, whether it's regular exercise, healthy eating, practicing gratitude, or dedicating time to pursue your passions. Create a plan and break it down into manageable steps, gradually integrating these new habits into your daily routine.

When letting go of old habits, be patient with yourself. Change takes time, and setbacks are a natural part of the process. Instead of beating yourself up over slip-ups, acknowledge them as opportunities for learning and growth. Celebrate small victories along the way and stay committed to the positive changes you are making.

Letting go can be challenging and emotionally taxing. It's important to cultivate self-compassion throughout this journey. Understand that letting go doesn't mean erasing the past or dismissing its significance. It means acknowledging that holding onto what no longer serves you limits your potential for happiness and growth. Treat yourself with kindness and understanding as you navigate the process of letting go, and remember that you deserve to live a life that aligns with your true self.

Letting go of what no longer serves you can be a transformative but sometimes daunting process. Surround yourself with a support system of friends, family, or even a professional therapist or coach who can provide guidance and encouragement. Sharing your experiences and emotions with others who understand can be immensely helpful in navigating the challenges of letting go.

Letting go of the things that no longer serve you is a courageous act that opens the door to new possibilities and personal growth. By recognizing what no longer aligns with your values, embracing impermanence, practicing mindfulness, decluttering physically and emotionally, shifting limiting beliefs, cultivating new habits, and nurturing self-compassion, you empower yourself to create a life that is truly fulfilling. Remember that letting go is an ongoing process, and as you continue to release what weighs you down, you create space for joy, growth, and an authentic expression of who you are. Trust in the journey and embrace the freedom that comes with letting go.

In life, we often find ourselves holding onto things that no longer serve us—beliefs, behaviors, relationships, and even aspects of our own identities. These attachments can hinder our progress, drain our energy, and prevent us from embracing new opportunities. In this chapter, we will delve deeper into the art of letting go, exploring why it is crucial for our personal growth and well-being. We will also provide practical strategies to help you release the things that no longer serve you, paving the way for a more fulfilling and authentic life.

To begin the process of letting go, take some time to reflect on your values and goals. What truly matters to you? Are your current attachments aligned with these values? Consider the aspects of your life that may be holding you back or causing you distress. By gaining clarity on what you truly value, you can better discern which elements no longer serve your greater purpose.

Emotional attachments can be deeply ingrained and challenging to release. Take a compassionate inventory of your emotions and identify any attachments that are no longer serving you. Are you holding onto grudges, regrets, or past traumas? Acknowledge the emotions associated with these attachments, and understand that by releasing them, you can free yourself from their negative influence.

Letting go requires acceptance and forgiveness— both for others and yourself. Acceptance means acknowledging that the past cannot be changed and that holding onto it only hampers your present and future. Similarly, forgiveness is an act of compassion, freeing yourself from the burden of resentment or anger. Practice acceptance and forgiveness, not to condone past actions, but to release their hold on your life.

Change is a constant in life, and clinging to familiarity can hinder our growth. Embrace the inevitability of change and develop a mindset that sees uncertainty as an opportunity for growth and new experiences. Understand that letting go often means stepping into the unknown, and that is where transformation can flourish.

Our relationships shape our lives, and it is essential to assess whether they are serving our well-being. Consider the people you surround yourself with—friends, romantic partners, colleagues—and evaluate how these relationships impact your happiness, growth, and values. Letting go of toxic or unfulfilling relationships can be difficult, but prioritizing your well-being is crucial for your personal development.

Our beliefs have a profound influence on our thoughts, actions, and experiences. Identify any limiting beliefs that are holding you back from reaching your full potential. Challenge these beliefs by seeking evidence to the contrary and reframing them into empowering and supportive beliefs. Let go of self-imposed limitations and embrace a mindset that empowers and uplifts you.

Letting go can be emotionally taxing, and it is vital to prioritize self-care and self-compassion throughout the process. Take care of your physical, emotional, and mental well-being. Practice self-compassion by treating yourself with kindness and understanding, especially when facing challenges or setbacks. Nurture yourself and create a supportive environment that encourages growth and healing.

Letting go is not solely about releasing what no longer serves you; it also involves creating space for the new and positive to enter your life. As you release attachments, consciously invite new experiences, relationships, and perspectives that align with your values and aspirations. Embrace the opportunities that arise and be open to the possibilities that come with letting go.

The human mind has a peculiar tendency to cling to the past, to wander through the corridors of memories and relive moments long gone. We find ourselves dwelling on past mistakes, lost opportunities, or the way things used to be. We become entangled in the web of nostalgia, constantly replaying events and conversations in our heads, wondering what could have been. But as we embark on a journey of self-discovery and growth, we come to realize that dwelling on the past never serves us. In fact, it hinders our progress and prevents us from fully embracing the present.

One of the reasons we often find ourselves stuck in the past is our desire to rewrite history, to change the outcome of past events. We falsely believe that by reliving those moments in our minds, we can somehow alter their course. However, the past is beyond our control. It has already happened, and no amount of rumination can change what has transpired. By dwelling on the past, we create an illusion of control that keeps us trapped in a cycle of regret and disappointment.

When our minds are preoccupied with the past, we miss out on the beauty and opportunities of the present moment. Life is a constant flow, an ever-changing tapestry of experiences, and by fixating on what has already happened, we neglect what is happening right now. The present is where we have the power to shape our lives, make choices, and create new memories. By dwelling on the past, we deny ourselves the chance to fully engage with the richness of life.

Regret is a heavy burden to carry. It weighs us down and prevents us from moving forward. When we continually revisit past mistakes or missed chances, we keep ourselves mired in negative emotions. Instead of learning from our experiences, we become trapped in a cycle of self-blame and what-ifs. Regret is a teacher, but its lessons can only be learned if we accept what has happened and use it as a catalyst for personal growth.

Life is transient, and everything in it is subject to change. Dwelling on the past keeps us anchored in a time that no longer exists. We must come to terms with the impermanence of all things and accept that the past is an integral part of our journey but not the destination. Just as a river flows, we too must let go and move forward. By accepting the fleeting nature of the past, we free ourselves to embrace the limitless potential of the present.

Mindfulness is the practice of being fully present in the current moment, without judgment or attachment. It is a powerful tool to counteract the pull of the past. By cultivating mindfulness, we train our minds to focus on the present, to observe our thoughts and emotions without getting entangled in them. Through mindfulness, we develop the ability to let go of the past and engage with life in its raw and unfiltered form.

Forgiveness is not about condoning or forgetting the past; it is about freeing ourselves from the burdens of resentment and anger. When we hold onto past hurts, we keep ourselves imprisoned in a cycle of pain. By forgiving others and ourselves, we break free from that cycle and open up space for healing and growth. Forgiveness is a profound act of self-love and an essential step toward letting go of the past.

The realization that dwelling on the past never serves us opens the door to embracing the power of now. The present moment is where our power resides—the power to make choices, to create meaningful connections, and to shape our lives. When we let go of the past, we tap into the abundance of possibilities that the present holds.

Embracing the power of now requires a shift in perspective. We start by acknowledging that the past is a part of our story, but it doesn't define us. We release the grip it has on our thoughts and emotions, understanding that the present is where true transformation happens.

Living in the present moment allows us to fully engage with our surroundings and the people in our lives. We become more attuned to the small wonders and joys that might have gone unnoticed while our minds were fixated on the past. By being present, we cultivate gratitude for what we have, fostering a sense of contentment and fulfillment.

In the present, we also find the opportunity to learn and grow. We draw lessons from past experiences, but we don't let them hold us back. Instead, we apply those lessons to make better choices and create a brighter future. Each moment becomes an opportunity for self-improvement and personal development.

Moreover, the present moment is where we can nurture and strengthen our relationships. When we are fully present with others, we listen attentively, empathize deeply, and connect authentically. By letting go of the past, we create space for new connections and deeper bonds to form.

Practicing mindfulness and self-awareness becomes essential in embracing the power of now. By being aware of our thoughts and emotions, we can catch ourselves when we start dwelling on the past and gently redirect our focus to the present. Mindfulness allows us to observe our experiences without judgment, cultivating a sense of peace and acceptance.

Letting go of the past doesn't mean disregarding the memories or lessons learned. It means releasing the grip of attachment and allowing ourselves to move forward. We honor the past by cherishing the positive experiences and integrating the lessons into our present lives.

As we continue to embrace the power of now, we realize that life is a dynamic and ever-changing journey. We understand that dwelling on the past only keeps us stagnant, while embracing the present propels us forward into a future filled with endless possibilities.

In conclusion, the realization that dwelling on the past never serves us opens the door to a more fulfilling and meaningful life. By letting go of what has already happened, we free ourselves from the burdens of regret and resentment. We learn to live in the present, where our power and potential lie. Embracing the power of now allows us to fully engage with life, cultivate mindfulness, nurture relationships, and create a future that aligns with our truest selves. Let go, embrace the present, and embark on a journey of growth, joy, and fulfillment.

Moving On

In the journey of life, we often find ourselves entangled in the webs of the past. Memories, regrets, and unhealed wounds can haunt our present and hinder our progress towards a brighter future. However, spiritual teachers and authors throughout history have emphasized the significance of moving on from the past. By releasing the burdens of yesterday, we open ourselves to new possibilities, personal growth, and profound transformation. Let us explore the wisdom of these enlightened souls and discover the importance of embracing the power of moving on.

"The past has no power over the present moment." - Eckhart Tolle

Eckhart Tolle, a renowned spiritual teacher, reminds us that dwelling on the past robs us of the only moment we truly have: the present. The past no longer exists except as memories or regrets within our minds. By fully engaging with the present moment, we free ourselves from the shackles of past experiences and open ourselves to the infinite potential of now.

"The only way out is through." - Robert Frost

Renowned poet Robert Frost beautifully encapsulates the essence of moving on. Sometimes, we may feel tempted to avoid confronting our past or burying our pain deep within ourselves. However, true healing lies in acknowledging and processing our emotions, allowing ourselves to go through the necessary steps of growth and self-discovery. Moving on requires courage and a willingness to face our past rather than escaping from it.

"You can't start the next chapter of your life if you keep re-reading the last one." - Michael McMillan

Michael McMillan, the author of "Paper Airplanes," poignantly reminds us that clinging to the past can hinder our progress. Each chapter of our lives holds valuable lessons, but if we constantly dwell on previous chapters, we deny ourselves the opportunity for personal evolution and the creation of a more fulfilling future. Moving on means turning the page, embracing change, and embarking on a new chapter with hope and anticipation.

"The truth is, unless you let go, unless you forgive yourself, unless you forgive the situation, unless you realize that the situation is over, you cannot move forward." - Steve Maraboli

Steve Maraboli, a behavioral scientist and author, emphasizes the importance of forgiveness and letting go. Holding onto past grievances, regrets, or self-blame can weigh heavily on our hearts and impede our progress. True liberation comes from forgiving ourselves, others, and the circumstances that have wounded us. Only then can we release the past and step forward with renewed vitality.

"You can't reach for anything new if your hands are still full of yesterday's junk." - Louise Smith

Louise Smith, a motivational speaker, encourages us to declutter our minds and hearts from the remnants of the past. Just as physical clutter can inhibit productivity and creativity, emotional clutter obstructs our ability to manifest new opportunities. Moving on necessitates releasing the attachment to outdated beliefs, relationships, and experiences that no longer serve our growth.

Spiritual teachers and authors have long emphasized the importance of moving on from the past. Through their timeless wisdom, we are reminded that we possess the power to release the burdens of yesterday and embrace the present moment with grace and resilience. By acknowledging the past, forgiving ourselves and others, and letting go of what no longer serves us, we unlock the gateway to personal growth, inner peace, and a brighter future. May we find the strength within ourselves to embark on this transformative journey of moving on, embracing the power of the present, and creating a life imbued with joy and fulfillment.

"The past is a place of reference, not a place of residence." - Unknown

This anonymous quote encapsulates the essence of the past's role in our lives. While the past holds valuable lessons and memories, it is not meant to be a permanent dwelling place. It is a reference point from which we can draw wisdom, but it should not define our present or restrict our future. By recognizing the past as a teacher rather than a captor, we can move on and make the most of the present moment.

"The art of life lies in a constant readjustment to our surroundings." - Kakuzo Okakura

Kakuzo Okakura, a Japanese author and scholar, highlights the importance of adaptability and flexibility in our journey through life. The past is a part of our surroundings, but dwelling on it excessively prevents us from adapting to the ever-changing circumstances of the present. Moving on requires a willingness to readjust our perspective, expectations, and actions to align with our current reality, enabling personal growth and resilience.

"Holding onto anger is like drinking poison and expecting the other person to die." - Gautama Buddha

The profound wisdom of Gautama Buddha reminds us of the toxic nature of holding onto negative emotions, particularly anger. When we cling to past grievances, we harm ourselves more than anyone else. Moving on involves releasing the grip of anger and resentment, allowing ourselves to experience peace and emotional well-being. By letting go of grudges, we liberate ourselves from the burdens of the past and create space for love, compassion, and forgiveness to flourish.

"The secret of change is to focus all of your energy not on fighting the old, but on building the new." - Socrates

Socrates, the ancient Greek philosopher, imparts invaluable advice on the transformative power of shifting our focus. Rather than investing our energy in resisting or dwelling on the past, we can redirect our efforts towards constructing a brighter future. Moving on requires embracing change, setting new goals, and channeling our energy towards positive endeavors that align with our aspirations. By actively building the new, we create a life filled with purpose and fulfillment.

"Every exit is an entry somewhere else." - Tom Stoppard

Tom Stoppard, a playwright, captures the essence of moving on as a doorway to new beginnings. When we close a chapter of our lives, it creates space for fresh opportunities and growth. Every ending becomes a gateway to a new phase, brimming with endless possibilities. Moving on involves recognizing that leaving the past behind opens doors to new experiences, relationships, and self-discovery.

The wisdom of spiritual teachers and authors teaches us that moving on from the past is essential for personal growth, resilience, and a fulfilling life. By recognizing the past as a reference point, adapting to our surroundings, and releasing negative emotions, we free ourselves to embrace change and construct a brighter future. Moving on requires courage, forgiveness, and a willingness to focus on the present moment and the limitless possibilities it holds. Let us heed the guidance of these enlightened souls and embark on the transformative journey of moving on, embracing the power of the now, and creating a life filled with joy, authenticity, and purpose.

"Don't let yesterday use up too much of today."
- Will Rogers

Will Rogers, an American humorist, reminds us of the importance of not allowing the past to consume our present. Dwelling on past mistakes, regrets, or missed opportunities only robs us of the precious time we have today. Moving on requires consciously redirecting our focus and energy towards the present moment, where we have the power to make positive changes and create a better future.

"The past is a ghost, the future a dream. All we ever have is now." - Bill Cosby

Bill Cosby's quote encapsulates the ephemeral nature of the past and future compared to the tangible reality of the present. The past is intangible, existing only as memories or ghosts in our minds. The future remains uncertain, existing only as dreams and possibilities. Moving on invites us to embrace the power of now, recognizing that it is the only moment in which we can truly live, take action, and shape our lives.

"If you are depressed, you are living in the past. If you are anxious, you are living in the future. If you are at peace, you are living in the present." - Lao Tzu

Lao Tzu, an ancient Chinese philosopher, offers profound insight into the connection between our mental state and our temporal focus. Dwelling on the past breeds depression, while fixating on the future breeds anxiety. Moving on entails finding peace and contentment in the present moment, where we can fully experience the beauty of life and engage with the world around us.

"Your task is not to seek for love, but merely to seek and find all the barriers within yourself that you have built against it." - Rumi

Rumi, a revered Persian poet and mystic, urges us to examine the barriers we have constructed within ourselves that prevent us from moving on and experiencing love fully. These barriers can include past traumas, unresolved emotions, or limiting beliefs. Moving on requires introspection, self-awareness, and the courage to dismantle these barriers, allowing love and healing to flow into our lives.

"Life moves on and so should we." - Spencer Johnson

Spencer Johnson, author of "Who Moved My Cheese?", emphasizes the inevitability of life's constant motion and the importance of adapting to it. Life is ever-changing, and holding onto the past stagnates our growth and hinders our ability to embrace new opportunities. Moving on invites us to flow with the natural rhythm of life, acknowledging that change is the only constant and embracing it with an open heart and mind.

The wisdom of spiritual teachers and authors teaches us that moving on from the past is not only vital but also liberating. By recognizing the fleeting nature of the past, redirecting our focus to the present, seeking peace within ourselves, and embracing life's changes, we can embark on a journey of personal growth, fulfillment, and authenticity. Moving on requires us to release the grip of the past, step boldly into the present, and trust in the unfolding of our future. Let us heed the guidance of these wise souls and embrace the transformative power of moving on, allowing us to live our lives to the fullest.

"The more you dwell in the past and future, the shorter your present moment becomes." - Sadhguru

Sadhguru, a contemporary spiritual teacher, draws our attention to the detrimental effects of excessive focus on the past and future. When we continuously dwell in memories or anxieties, we rob ourselves of fully experiencing the present moment. Moving on invites us to cultivate mindfulness and be fully present, expanding the richness of each passing moment and gaining a deeper connection to ourselves and the world around us.

"In the process of letting go, you will lose many things from the past, but you will find yourself." - Deepak Chopra

Deepak Chopra, a renowned author and spiritual teacher, illuminates the transformative nature of letting go. Moving on necessitates releasing attachments to the past, whether they are material possessions, outdated beliefs, or past identities. In this process, we shed layers that no longer serve us, unveiling the true essence of who we are. Moving on becomes a journey of self-discovery and self-realization, allowing us to align with our authentic selves.

"The past cannot be changed. The future is yet in your power." - Unknown

This anonymous quote serves as a powerful reminder that our power lies in the present moment and the choices we make moving forward. While we cannot alter the past, we have the ability to shape our future through the actions, decisions, and mindset we embrace today. Moving on requires embracing our agency and taking responsibility for creating a future that aligns with our desires and aspirations.

"Your present circumstances don't determine where you can go; they merely determine where you start." - Nido Qubein

Nido Qubein, a motivational speaker and author, emphasizes that our current circumstances should not limit our potential or hold us captive to the past. Moving on invites us to view our present circumstances as a starting point for growth and transformation. Regardless of our past experiences or current challenges, we possess the power to forge a new path and create a future that surpasses our wildest dreams.

"Letting go doesn't mean that you forget or erase the past; it means that you choose to stop living in it." - Unknown

This final quote, of unknown origin, encapsulates the essence of moving on. Letting go does not imply disregarding the past or erasing its significance but rather choosing not to dwell in it. Moving on means embracing the present and future with open arms, acknowledging the past as part of our story but not allowing it to define or confine us. It is a conscious decision to release the weight of the past and step into a new chapter of our lives.

The teachings of spiritual teachers and authors emphasize that moving on is a transformative journey that allows us to fully embrace the present moment, discover our true selves, and shape our future. By staying present, letting go of attachments, realizing our power to create change, and choosing to live in the now, we free ourselves from the constraints of the past and open ourselves to infinite possibilities. Moving on invites us to embark on a path of personal growth, self-discovery, and fulfillment, enabling us to live life to its fullest potential.

Human beings are inherently shaped by their past experiences. Our memories and interactions with the world play a vital role in shaping our identity and influencing our future actions. Understanding the psychology of learning from our past can empower us to make better decisions, grow personally and professionally, and navigate life's challenges with greater wisdom and resilience. In this chapter, we delve into the intricate workings of the human mind and explore how we can harness the power of our past to shape a brighter future.

Memory serves as the foundation for learning from our past. Our brains are remarkable storage systems that collect, encode, and retrieve information about our experiences. Memories can be short-term or long-term, and their formation is influenced by various factors such as emotional intensity, repetition, and personal relevance.

Emotional experiences have a profound impact on memory formation. Events that elicit strong emotions, whether positive or negative, tend to be remembered more vividly. This phenomenon, known as the emotional memory effect, can be attributed to the amygdala's involvement, a brain region responsible for processing emotions. By recognizing the emotional significance of past events, we can gain insight into our behavioral patterns and motivations.

The process of recalling memories is not always accurate or objective. Our minds often engage in selective recall, focusing on particular details or events that align with our preexisting beliefs or emotional states. This bias can lead to distortions in our perception of the past and hinder our ability to learn effectively. Recognizing this tendency and actively seeking diverse perspectives can help us overcome these limitations and gain a more comprehensive understanding of our past experiences.

Learning from the past involves extracting valuable lessons from our experiences. Reflection and introspection play a crucial role in this process. By taking the time to analyze our actions, choices, and outcomes, we can identify patterns, strengths, and areas for improvement. This self-awareness allows us to make informed decisions in the present and avoid repeating past mistakes.

Developing a growth mindset is essential for learning from the past. Embracing the belief that our abilities and intelligence can be developed through effort and learning enables us to view failures and setbacks as opportunities for growth. By reframing failures as stepping stones rather than insurmountable obstacles, we cultivate resilience and a willingness to learn from our past experiences.

Regret is a common emotion associated with learning from the past. While regret can be a powerful motivator for change, dwelling excessively on past mistakes can be detrimental to our well-being. It is crucial to strike a balance between acknowledging regrets, extracting lessons, and moving forward. Practicing self-compassion and forgiveness allows us to release the burden of regret and embrace the potential for personal growth.

Learning from our past experiences enhances our decision-making abilities. By drawing upon the knowledge and insights gained from past successes and failures, we can make more informed choices and mitigate potential risks. Reflecting on the consequences of past decisions helps us assess the potential outcomes of our current choices, increasing our chances of achieving desired goals.

The psychology of learning from our past is a dynamic process that involves memory, emotional significance, selective recall, self-reflection, and a growth mindset. By understanding the intricacies of our own minds and actively engaging with our past experiences, we can navigate the present with greater wisdom and shape a future that aligns with our aspirations. Embracing the lessons and growth opportunities presented by our past empowers us to live more intentionally and create a fulfilling and purposeful life.

Life is a journey filled with ups and downs, victories and setbacks. Throughout our lives, we encounter various challenges that test our resilience and determination. Moving forward in life requires a deep understanding of our psychology, as it plays a vital role in shaping our ability to overcome obstacles and embrace new opportunities. In this chapter, we will explore the psychology behind moving forward, drawing insights from clinical studies that shed light on the human mind's capacity for growth, adaptation, and transformation.

Psychologist Carol Dweck introduced the concept of a growth mindset, which suggests that individuals who believe their abilities and intelligence can be developed through effort and learning are more likely to succeed. In a landmark study conducted by Dweck and her colleagues, it was found that individuals with a growth mindset were more resilient, performed better in challenging situations, and were more likely to persevere in the face of setbacks. By adopting a growth mindset, we can cultivate an attitude of continuous improvement, which is crucial for moving forward in life.

Resilience is the psychological capacity to bounce back from adversity and maintain a positive outlook despite challenging circumstances. Researchers have extensively studied resilience and identified several factors that contribute to its development. One such factor is the presence of a strong support network. Studies have shown that individuals with close relationships, be it friends, family, or mentors, are more likely to navigate through difficult times successfully. Additionally, cultivating effective coping strategies, such as reframing negative events and practicing self-care, can enhance resilience and enable us to move forward with greater ease.

Life is inherently dynamic, and embracing change is an essential component of moving forward. Psychologists have examined the process of change and its impact on our well-being. Studies have shown that individuals who approach change with an open mind and view it as an opportunity for growth experience higher levels of life satisfaction and overall psychological well-being. Moreover, research suggests that engaging in new experiences and stepping outside of our comfort zones promotes personal growth and enhances psychological flexibility, enabling us to adapt and progress in life.

Goal-setting is a fundamental psychological process that propels us forward. Clinical studies have highlighted the importance of setting meaningful and realistic goals in driving motivation and providing a sense of purpose. The well-known theory of goal-setting developed by psychologist Edwin Locke and his colleagues suggests that specific and challenging goals lead to higher levels of performance and greater personal satisfaction. When we set goals aligned with our values and aspirations, we create a roadmap for progress and provide ourselves with a sense of direction in moving forward.

Fear and self-doubt often hinder our ability to move forward in life. Clinical research in the field of cognitive-behavioral therapy (CBT) has demonstrated that challenging irrational beliefs and negative thought patterns can lead to significant improvements in overall well-being. By identifying and reframing self-limiting beliefs, we can overcome fear and self-doubt, paving the way for personal growth and progress.

Moving forward in life requires an understanding of the psychology that underlies our thoughts, emotions, and behaviors. By cultivating a growth mindset, developing resilience, embracing change, setting meaningful goals, and addressing fear and self-doubt, we can navigate the challenges that come our way and move forward with confidence. Clinical studies have provided valuable insights into these psychological processes, offering us evidence-based strategies to overcome obstacles, adapt to new situations, and create a fulfilling life journey. Remember, moving forward is not just about reaching a destination but embracing the transformative power of the journey itself.

Evaluating Ownership

You did it. It happened. It wasn't an accident or a coincidence. It was a planned, well-thought-out choice. It's time to own your decision.

Conquering your past will demand you own your past. And that you own it in its entirety. For far too long you've told the amended, shortened version of events – the version that seems less messy. It's time to become more authentic when speaking of your past. It's time to take ownership. Until you do, it will plague you.

In the realm of human experience, vulnerability is often associated with weakness, fragility, and exposure. It is a state of being that strips away our defenses and leaves us open to potential harm. While vulnerability can be seen as a fundamental aspect of our existence, it also carries with it a certain element of horror. In this chapter, we will explore the unsettling aspects of vulnerability and how it can evoke fear and terror within us.

One of the most horrifying aspects of vulnerability is its inherent unpredictability. When we let our guards down and allow ourselves to be vulnerable, we enter into uncharted territory. We expose ourselves to the unknown, relinquishing control over the outcomes of our actions. This lack of certainty can be deeply unsettling, as it opens the door to potential pain, rejection, or betrayal. The fear of the unexpected and the inability to foresee the consequences can fuel our anxieties and amplify the horror of vulnerability.

Emotional vulnerability, in particular, can be an intensely horrifying experience. When we allow ourselves to be emotionally open and honest, we expose our deepest fears, desires, and insecurities to others. This raw authenticity can make us feel naked, as if our innermost selves are laid bare for scrutiny. The fear of being judged, ridiculed, or rejected for our true emotions can create a sense of terror that makes vulnerability an inherently dreadful prospect.

Vulnerability can also become horrifying when it intersects with power imbalances and exploitation. When we are vulnerable, we often rely on others for support, understanding, or protection. However, this reliance can be exploited by those who seek to take advantage of our vulnerability. The realization that our trust can be manipulated and abused can be deeply disturbing. The horror lies in the betrayal of our vulnerability, as it reminds us of the dark side of human nature and the potential for harm lurking within others.

Another terror-inducing aspect of vulnerability is the fear of rejection and isolation. When we open ourselves up to others, we become susceptible to their judgments and rejections. The prospect of being cast aside, abandoned, or ostracized can be agonizing. Humans are inherently social beings, and the fear of being left alone, disconnected from the support and validation of others, can be a source of profound horror. The vulnerability that comes with seeking connection and belonging can make us acutely aware of our fragile place in the social fabric.

Vulnerability is closely intertwined with loss and grief. When we form deep connections with others or invest ourselves fully in endeavors and aspirations, we expose ourselves to the possibility of loss. The awareness that what we hold dear can be taken away from us can be terrifying. The pain and anguish associated with loss can make vulnerability an unwelcome companion, evoking a sense of dread and apprehension.

While vulnerability is an essential part of the human experience, it can also be a source of horror. The unpredictability, emotional exposedness, power imbalances, fear of rejection, and vulnerability to loss all contribute to the unsettling nature of vulnerability. Recognizing and understanding these aspects can help us navigate the treacherous terrain of vulnerability and find ways to embrace it without succumbing to overwhelming fear.

Vulnerability has an intimate relationship with shame, which can intensify its horrifying nature. When we expose our vulnerabilities, we risk facing judgment and criticism from others. The fear of being seen as flawed, weak, or inadequate can trigger deep feelings of shame. The horror lies in the potential humiliation and self-deprecation that vulnerability can bring, leaving us feeling exposed and unworthy.

In certain situations, vulnerability can be a precursor to trauma, adding an even more sinister dimension to its horror. When individuals find themselves in vulnerable positions, whether due to their circumstances or the actions of others, they become susceptible to traumatic experiences. The fear of enduring physical, emotional, or psychological harm amplifies the terror associated with vulnerability, as it represents a direct threat to one's well-being and sense of safety.

One of the most disconcerting aspects of vulnerability is the loss of control that accompanies it. When we allow ourselves to be vulnerable, we surrender a certain level of power and autonomy. This loss of control can be deeply unsettling, as it leaves us at the mercy of external forces. The horror lies in the realization that vulnerability makes us vulnerable to manipulation, exploitation, and unforeseen consequences, eroding our sense of agency and amplifying feelings of helplessness.

Intimacy requires vulnerability, as it involves revealing our true selves to another person. While intimacy can be beautiful and fulfilling, it also carries an inherent horror. Opening up to someone at a profound level means risking emotional harm and the potential for betrayal. The fear of being emotionally wounded by someone we trust can make vulnerability within intimate relationships a deeply unsettling and terrifying experience.

At its core, vulnerability forces us to confront our mortality and the fragile nature of our existence. The awareness that we are susceptible to pain, loss, and ultimately, our own mortality, can generate existential dread. The horror lies in the vulnerability of being human, in the recognition that life is transient and unpredictable. This existential aspect of vulnerability can instill a profound sense of dread, reminding us of our own limitations and the fleeting nature of our time on Earth.

Vulnerability can be horrifying due to its unpredictability, emotional exposedness, power imbalances, fear of rejection, vulnerability to loss and grief, shame, trauma, loss of control, the vulnerability of intimacy, and the existential dread it evokes. While vulnerability may be frightening, it is an integral part of the human experience. By acknowledging and understanding the horrors associated with vulnerability, we can navigate its challenges with greater resilience, empathy, and self-compassion. Embracing vulnerability, despite its terrors, allows us to forge genuine connections, foster personal growth, and ultimately live more authentic and fulfilling lives.

Life is a journey filled with ups and downs, victories and defeats, and moments of joy and regret. As we navigate through this intricate web of experiences, it is essential to acknowledge that our past shapes who we are today. Taking responsibility for our actions and owning our past is not an easy task, but it is a necessary step towards personal growth, healing, and creating a better future. In this chapter, we will explore the transformative power of accepting responsibility, learning from mistakes, and embracing the person we have become.

Our past is a culmination of the choices we have made, whether good or bad. By accepting that we had the power of choice, we reclaim control over our lives. It is easy to fall into the trap of blaming external circumstances or other people for our misfortunes, but true empowerment lies in recognizing that we had agency in those moments. By taking responsibility, we free ourselves from the chains of victimhood and open the door to personal growth.

Mistakes are an inevitable part of the human experience. Rather than avoiding or denying them, we should confront our mistakes head-on. Owning our past means acknowledging our wrongdoings, understanding the impact they had on ourselves and others, and learning from them. Each mistake is an opportunity for growth and self-improvement. By reflecting on our actions, we gain valuable insights that guide us towards making better choices in the future.

Taking responsibility also involves forgiveness. It is important to forgive ourselves for the mistakes we have made and the pain we have caused. Holding onto guilt and shame only perpetuates the cycle of negativity, preventing us from moving forward. Additionally, forgiveness extends to others who may have wronged us in the past. By releasing the burden of resentment, we open up space for healing and create an environment conducive to personal transformation.

Owning our past requires us to be honest with ourselves and others. It means embracing our vulnerabilities and imperfections, allowing us to connect more deeply with ourselves and those around us. By acknowledging our past openly and authentically, we invite others to do the same, fostering a sense of trust and understanding. When we are transparent about our past, we can build stronger relationships and create a support system that encourages personal growth.

Taking responsibility is not just about acknowledging our past; it is about taking action to make amends. If we have caused harm to others, it is crucial to take the necessary steps to apologize, seek forgiveness, and rectify the situation to the best of our abilities. Actions speak louder than words, and by actively working towards making things right, we demonstrate our commitment to personal growth and accountability.

Owning our past does not mean dwelling in it indefinitely. It is a crucial stepping stone towards personal growth and building a better future. Once we have taken responsibility, learned from our mistakes, and made amends, we can shift our focus to the present moment and the possibilities that lie ahead. Our past does not define us entirely; it is merely a chapter in our story. By embracing growth, we can create a brighter future filled with purpose, resilience, and fulfillment.

Taking responsibility and owning our past is a transformative process that requires courage, introspection, and a commitment to personal growth. By embracing the power of choice, learning from mistakes, and forgiving ourselves and others, we can release the shackles of the past and step into a future filled with newfound wisdom and empowerment. As we embark on this journey of self-discovery, let us reflect on our past with honesty, make amends where necessary, and embrace the growth that comes from taking ownership of our lives. Remember, the past does not define us, but it does shape us. By taking responsibility, we reclaim our agency and create a foundation for a brighter future.

While taking responsibility is essential, it is equally important to cultivate self-compassion throughout this process. It is easy to be overly critical of ourselves when facing our past mistakes or shortcomings. However, true growth and healing come from a place of self-love and understanding. Treat yourself with kindness, acknowledging that you are human and bound to make mistakes. Embrace self-forgiveness and use it as a catalyst for growth, allowing yourself to move forward with a renewed sense of purpose.

Owning our past can be a challenging and sometimes overwhelming journey. It is crucial to seek support from trusted friends, family members, or professionals who can provide guidance and a non-judgmental space for reflection. Surround yourself with individuals who encourage your growth and hold you accountable for your actions. A support system not only provides perspective and guidance but also helps us stay committed to the path of personal transformation.

Taking responsibility for your past allows you to rewrite your narrative. Instead of letting your past define you, embrace the opportunity to redefine who you are and who you want to become. Use the lessons learned from your past experiences to shape a new vision for your future. You have the power to change, grow, and create a life that aligns with your values and aspirations. By owning your past, you gain the freedom to create a new story, one that reflects your true potential.

Gratitude is a powerful tool in the journey of owning your past. Even amidst difficult experiences or mistakes, there are always lessons and moments of growth to be grateful for. Embrace gratitude for the opportunities to learn, evolve, and make amends. Cultivating a mindset of gratitude allows you to shift your focus from dwelling on the past to appreciating the present moment and the possibilities that lie ahead.

Taking responsibility and owning our past is a transformative process that requires courage, self-reflection, and a willingness to grow. It is through this process that we release ourselves from the burdens of guilt and shame, and we empower ourselves to create a future filled with authenticity, compassion, and personal fulfillment. Remember, you have the power to shape your narrative and embrace the lessons from your past to create a life that reflects your truest self.

In life, we are constantly faced with choices and decisions that shape our experiences and interactions with others. Sometimes, these choices lead to positive outcomes, while at other times, they may result in negative consequences or harm. Taking accountability for our actions is an essential aspect of personal growth and responsibility. It means acknowledging and owning up to the impact of our choices, both positive and negative, and actively working to make amends and learn from our mistakes. In this chapter, we will explore what it truly means to take accountability for your actions and why it is a crucial aspect of personal development.

To take accountability for your actions, the first step is to recognize and acknowledge what you have done. This involves honestly assessing the situation, understanding the impact of your choices, and accepting your role in the outcome. It requires looking beyond any justifications or excuses and taking an objective view of the situation. By being self-aware and accepting responsibility for your actions, you demonstrate maturity and a willingness to face the consequences.

Every action we take has consequences, and taking accountability means understanding and accepting those consequences. It involves recognizing how our choices affect others, whether positively or negatively. By understanding the impact of our actions, we become more mindful of our behavior and its potential ramifications. This awareness enables us to make more informed choices in the future and strive for positive outcomes.

One of the most challenging but crucial aspects of taking accountability is owning up to our mistakes. It means admitting when we have made an error, regardless of how uncomfortable or embarrassing it may be. Owning up to our mistakes requires humility and the ability to put our ego aside. By acknowledging our shortcomings and accepting responsibility, we demonstrate integrity and earn the respect of others.

When we take accountability for our actions, it is essential to make amends whenever possible. This involves actively seeking to repair the damage caused by our behavior and taking steps to rectify the situation. Making amends can vary depending on the circumstances, but it may involve offering a sincere apology, compensating for any losses or harm inflicted, or actively working to change our behavior for the better. By taking these steps, we demonstrate our commitment to growth and learning from our mistakes.

Present Grace

In our journey of personal growth and self-discovery, one of the most profound and challenging aspects we encounter is the need to confront and overcome our pasts. Whether we carry emotional scars from past traumas, harbor regrets about past mistakes, or struggle with self-forgiveness, the process of healing requires us to extend grace to ourselves. This chapter explores the transformative power of allowing ourselves grace as we navigate the intricate path of overcoming our pasts.

Our pasts, though intangible, have a tremendous impact on our present and future. They shape our beliefs, attitudes, and behaviors, influencing our relationships and the way we perceive ourselves.

However, it's crucial to recognize that our pasts do not define us entirely. We are not bound by our mistakes, shortcomings, or painful experiences. Instead, we have the capacity to grow, learn, and evolve beyond our pasts.

When we carry the weight of our pasts, it's easy to fall into the trap of self-judgment. We may replay our mistakes and failures in our minds, creating a cycle of negativity that hinders our progress. It is vital to acknowledge that we are human, prone to imperfections, and that our pasts do not reflect our worth or potential. Recognizing this truth is the first step towards embracing grace.

Self-compassion is the cornerstone of granting ourselves grace. It involves treating ourselves with kindness, understanding, and empathy. Instead of berating ourselves for our past actions, we must strive to offer compassion and forgiveness. We can start by acknowledging that we did the best we could with the knowledge and resources we had at that time. It's essential to remember that growth and change are ongoing processes, and we deserve compassion as we navigate them.

Rather than viewing our pasts as a source of shame, we can reframe them as opportunities for growth. Our mistakes and challenges are not indicators of failure but rather stepping stones toward becoming the best versions of ourselves. Every setback, every misstep, can be seen as a lesson learned and a chance to gain wisdom and resilience. By embracing our imperfections, we unlock the transformative power of growth, allowing ourselves to transcend our pasts.

Forgiveness is a transformative act that sets us free from the burden of our pasts. It begins with forgiving ourselves. We must release the self-blame, guilt, and shame that may have consumed us for far too long. Forgiving ourselves doesn't mean condoning our past actions but rather acknowledging our capacity to change and grow. It's a conscious decision to let go of the past and embrace a future filled with self-love and acceptance.

Overcoming our pasts is a challenging journey that requires support and understanding. It's crucial to seek out and surround ourselves with people who uplift and encourage us. Whether it's friends, family, mentors, or support groups, having a strong support system provides the necessary guidance, empathy, and accountability as we navigate our healing process. Together, we can reinforce the idea that grace is a gift we all deserve.

As we embark on the path of overcoming our pasts, it's essential to move forward with intention. We can create a vision for the future we desire, setting meaningful goals and taking actionable steps to achieve them. By focusing on the present moment and aligning our actions with our values, we can gradually leave behind the weight of our pasts.

Grace allows us to make peace with our pasts, to heal old wounds, and to embrace a future filled with hope and possibility. Here are some practical strategies for cultivating grace as we continue on our journey of overcoming our pasts:

Develop a practice of mindfulness to observe your thoughts and emotions without judgment. When negative self-talk or feelings of guilt arise, acknowledge them, but don't let them define you. Cultivate self-awareness and recognize that you have the power to choose how you respond to your past.

Challenge negative beliefs about yourself and your past by reframing them with more compassionate and empowering narratives. Look for the lessons learned, the strengths gained, and the resilience that emerged from your experiences. Shift your focus from what went wrong to what you can do differently moving forward.

Prioritize self-care as an essential component of your healing process. Engage in activities that nurture your physical, mental, and emotional well-being. This may include exercise, healthy eating, getting enough rest, spending time in nature, practicing relaxation techniques, or engaging in creative outlets that bring you joy.

If you find it challenging to navigate the process of overcoming your past alone, don't hesitate to seek professional help. Therapists, counselors, or coaches can provide valuable guidance, support, and tools tailored to your specific needs. They can assist you in uncovering deeper layers of healing and help you develop healthy coping mechanisms.

Forgiveness is a profound act of grace that liberates both ourselves and others. It's a process that takes time and effort. Start by acknowledging the pain caused by others and yourself, and then make a conscious decision to release the resentment and anger. Remember that forgiveness is not condoning the actions; it is choosing to let go and move forward.

Overcoming our pasts often requires us to face our vulnerabilities and be honest with ourselves and others. Embrace vulnerability as a strength rather than a weakness. Share your story with trusted individuals who can provide support and validation. This openness allows for deeper connections and reinforces the understanding that we are not alone in our struggles.

Acknowledge and celebrate every step of progress you make, no matter how small. Recognize that healing is not linear and that setbacks may occur along the way. Embrace those setbacks as opportunities for further growth and continue moving forward with resilience and determination.

Allowing ourselves grace on the journey of overcoming our pasts is an act of self-love and acceptance. It empowers us to release the shackles of guilt, shame, and self-judgment, and to embrace a future filled with compassion, growth, and transformation. By cultivating grace, practicing self-compassion, and surrounding ourselves with support, we can navigate our healing process with resilience and move towards a life of authenticity, purpose, and inner peace.

Establishing healthy boundaries is crucial when overcoming our pasts. Identify behaviors, relationships, or situations that trigger negative emotions or hinder your progress. Learn to assertively communicate your needs and limits, and surround yourself with people who respect and support your boundaries. Creating a safe space for yourself allows room for healing and growth.

Gratitude is a powerful practice that can shift our focus from dwelling on the past to appreciating the present. Each day, take a moment to reflect on the things you are grateful for, no matter how small they may seem. Cultivating gratitude helps rewire our minds to recognize the beauty and positivity in our lives, fostering a sense of grace and contentment.

Seek inspiration from individuals who have overcome their own pasts and achieved personal growth. Read books, listen to podcasts, or attend workshops by people who have walked a similar path. Learning from their experiences and witnessing their resilience can provide guidance, encouragement, and a renewed sense of hope.

Engage in regular self-reflection to gain deeper insights into your past experiences and their impact on your present. Journaling, meditation, or engaging in therapy can facilitate this process. Explore your emotions, beliefs, and patterns of behavior with curiosity and compassion. Self-reflection allows you to identify areas for growth, make conscious choices, and move forward with clarity.

While it is important to acknowledge and learn from our pasts, it is equally important to embrace the present moment. The past is unchangeable, and the future is yet to come. By grounding ourselves in the present, we can fully experience life, make conscious choices, and shape our future with intention. Embracing the present moment allows us to let go of regrets and worries, and focus on what we can control now.

Instead of seeking external validation, work on cultivating self-validation. Recognize your worth and acknowledge your progress. Celebrate your achievements, no matter how small, and remind yourself that you are deserving of love, forgiveness, and grace. Trust in your ability to heal, grow, and create a brighter future.

Healing from our pasts is not an overnight process. It requires patience and kindness towards ourselves. Understand that there will be ups and downs along the way, and that setbacks are a natural part of the journey. Treat yourself with gentleness and compassion, just as you would a dear friend going through a similar experience.

Adopt a growth mindset that views challenges and setbacks as opportunities for growth and learning. Embrace the belief that you have the capacity to change and evolve, regardless of your past experiences. Shift your perspective from a fixed mindset that believes you are defined by your past, to a growth mindset that empowers you to create a better future.

Remember, the path of overcoming our pasts is unique to each individual. Be patient with yourself and trust that you have the strength and resilience to navigate this journey. By allowing ourselves grace, we open the door to healing, transformation, and a future filled with limitless possibilities.

In the journey of life, we all encounter situations and make choices that leave lasting imprints on our hearts and minds. These experiences can be filled with joy and triumph, but they can also be accompanied by regret, guilt, and shame. We often find ourselves caught in a web of negative emotions, unable to break free and move forward. However, there is a powerful tool that has the potential to liberate us from this cycle of self-condemnation: self-forgiveness.

When we dwell on past mistakes or harbor guilt, we carry an invisible burden that hinders our growth and happiness. The weight of regret consumes our thoughts, eroding our self-esteem and preventing us from embracing the present moment. To release this burden, we must acknowledge that we are imperfect beings capable of making errors.

It is essential to recognize that every person, without exception, makes mistakes. No one is exempt from experiencing missteps, poor judgments, or wrong choices. Embracing our imperfections allows us to connect with our shared humanity, fostering empathy not only for ourselves but also for others who have stumbled along their own paths.

Self-forgiveness requires honest self-reflection. We must be willing to confront our past actions and take responsibility for their consequences. Instead of shying away from our mistakes, we must examine them with a compassionate lens, understanding the context and circumstances that influenced our decisions. By accepting our past, we pave the way for personal growth and transformation.

Every misstep holds within it valuable lessons. Through self-forgiveness, we acknowledge that mistakes are opportunities for growth and development. By extracting wisdom from our experiences, we equip ourselves with the tools to make better choices in the future. Remember, the greatest triumphs often arise from the ashes of our most significant setbacks.

Self-forgiveness is intimately connected to self-compassion. Just as we would extend empathy and understanding to a friend in need, we must learn to treat ourselves with the same kindness. Embrace the truth that you deserve forgiveness, and acknowledge that healing begins within. Practice self-care, engage in positive self-talk, and nurture a loving relationship with yourself.

Forgiveness liberates us from the chains of the past. To truly move forward, we must let go of resentment and bitterness. This process involves making a conscious choice to release the negative emotions that bind us. Understand that forgiving yourself does not mean forgetting or condoning your actions; it means relinquishing the emotional hold they have on your present and future.

Self-forgiveness is not a one-time event but rather an ongoing process. As we navigate through life, we will continue to face challenges and encounter new opportunities for growth. Embrace the journey of personal transformation, recognizing that forgiveness is an integral part of our evolution. Celebrate your progress and use your newfound wisdom to create a brighter future.

Self-forgiveness is a powerful tool that empowers us to release the shackles of the past and embrace the beauty of the present moment. It is a gift we give ourselves, a healing balm for the wounds we carry within. By acknowledging our imperfections, reflecting on our actions, and cultivating self-compassion, we can pave the way for personal growth and transformation. As we let go of regret and resentment, we open ourselves to a future filled with joy, peace, and limitless possibilities. Remember, forgiving yourself is an act of courage, strength, and love— a profound act that sets you free from the chains of self-condemnation.

In the process of self-forgiveness, it's important to remember that it doesn't happen overnight. It requires patience, persistence, and a genuine commitment to your own healing and well-being. Be gentle with yourself as you navigate this journey, for healing takes time and effort.

One effective strategy in the practice of self-forgiveness is writing a forgiveness letter to yourself. Take a pen and paper, or open a blank document on your computer, and begin to pour out your feelings and thoughts. Acknowledge the mistakes you've made, express your remorse, and seek forgiveness from yourself. Write with authenticity, allowing yourself to be vulnerable and honest.

As you write, focus on shifting your perspective from self-blame to self-compassion. Remind yourself that you are a complex human being, capable of both great triumphs and regrettable actions. Embrace the understanding that mistakes are an integral part of growth and learning, and that they don't define your worth as a person.

Once you've completed your forgiveness letter, take a moment to read it aloud. Hear the words resonate in the air, and let their meaning sink into your soul. As you do so, visualize the weight of guilt and regret being lifted from your shoulders, replaced by a sense of peace and liberation.

Remember that self-forgiveness is not about erasing the past, but about making peace with it. It's about granting yourself permission to move forward and create a future that aligns with your values and aspirations. Embrace the lessons learned from your past experiences, for they have shaped you into the resilient individual you are today.

In addition to writing a forgiveness letter, practicing self-care and self-compassion is crucial in the process of self-forgiveness. Engage in activities that bring you joy, nurture your well-being, and promote self-reflection. Seek support from trusted friends, family members, or even professional counselors who can guide you through this transformative journey.

It's important to recognize that setbacks may occur along the way. You may find yourself slipping back into self-blame or experiencing moments of doubt. Be kind to yourself during these times, offering understanding and forgiveness for any lapses. Remember that self-forgiveness is a continuous process, and every step forward is a step toward healing.

As you embark on the path of self-forgiveness, be open to the possibilities of personal growth and renewal. Embrace the newfound freedom that comes from releasing yourself from the chains of the past. Allow self-forgiveness to be a catalyst for positive change in your life, empowering you to create a future filled with love, compassion, and self-acceptance.

Self-forgiveness is an essential practice for moving on from the past. It requires a willingness to let go of regret, embrace self-compassion, and actively work towards healing. By acknowledging your imperfections, learning from your mistakes, and practicing self-care, you can liberate yourself from the burden of self-condemnation and create a future filled with self-love and growth. Embrace the transformative power of self-forgiveness and embark on a journey of healing and liberation today.

Closing Thoughts

In the tapestry of life, there are moments that define us, moments that test our resilience, and moments that reveal our true character. It is in these moments that the human spirit yearns for redemption and the chance to start anew.

Life has a peculiar way of guiding us down unforeseen paths, often leading to places we never intended to go. You, my friend, deserve redemption. And in your darkest hours, a flicker of hope emerges, urging you to confront your shortcomings and seek a new beginning. And it is with this newfound clarity that you stand here today, ready to embrace redemption and carve a path toward a better future.

Deserving a second chance is not a proclamation; it is a personal journey defined by introspection, remorse, and a sincere commitment to change. It begins with acknowledging the mistakes of the past, accepting responsibility for the consequences they have wrought, and recognizing the pain you may have caused others along the way. You have come to understand the importance of empathy, compassion, and the capacity to make amends for the hurt you have inflicted upon others.

But mere acknowledgement is not enough. To deserve a second chance, you must actively engage in self-reflection and personal growth. You have spent countless hours dissecting your actions, dissecting the underlying motives that led you astray. Through this process, you have gained invaluable insight into the flaws that once defined you and have come to embrace the transformative power of change. You are now committed to cultivating a better version of yourself—a version that is grounded in integrity, resilience, and a genuine desire to make amends.

Redemption is not a solitary endeavor; it requires the support and understanding of those who have been impacted by your past actions. It is an invitation to bridge the chasm between your past self and the person you aspire to become. You are now prepared to engage in open and honest conversations, to listen to the perspectives of others, and to offer sincere apologies to those you have wronged. You are aware that rebuilding trust is a delicate process, one that demands patience, consistency, and a steadfast commitment to change.

You are not defined by the mistakes of your past, but rather by the lessons they have imparted. They have shaped you, molded you into someone who is ready to embark on a new journey, guided by wisdom and a profound appreciation for the gift of a second chance. You have learned that resilience is not merely bouncing back from failure; it is the ability to rise above adversity, to grow stronger in the face of challenges, and to emerge as a beacon of hope and inspiration for others who may be traversing a similar path.

Deserving a second chance in life is not an entitlement; it is a privilege. It is an opportunity to embrace the power of transformation, to transcend the limitations of the past, and to redefine one's destiny.

ABOUT THE AUTHOR

Dr. Jeremy Lopez is Founder and President of Identity Network and Now Is Your Moment. Identity Network is one of the world's leading prophetic resource sites, offering books, teachings, and courses to a global audience. For more than thirty years, Dr. Lopez has been considered a pioneering voice within the field of the prophetic arts and his proven strategies for success coaching are now being implemented by various training groups and faith groups throughout the world. Dr. Lopez is the author of more than forty books, including his international bestselling books The Universe is at Your Command and Creating with Your Thoughts. Throughout his career, he has spoken prophetically into the lives of heads of business as well as heads of state. He has ministered to Governor Bob Riley of the State of Alabama, Prime Minister Benjamin Netanyahu, and Shimon Peres. Dr. Lopez continues to be a highly sought conference teacher and host, speaking on the topics of human potential and spirituality.

ADDITIONAL WORKS

Prophetic Transformation

The Universe is at Your Command: Vibrating the Creative Side of God

Creating with Your Thoughts

Creating Your Soul Map: Manifesting the Future You with a Vision Board

Creating   Your   Soul   Map: A Visionary Workbook

Abandoned to Divine Destiny

The Law of Attraction: Universal   Power of Spirit

The Gospel of Manipulation

SEERS: The Eyes of the Kingdom

PROPHETIC READINGS

What is the Holy Spirit speaking to you in this season of your life? Find out by scheduling your very own personal and private prophetic reading with Prophet Jeremy Lopez. Contact the offices of Identity Network International by visiting www.identitynetwork.net.

DREAM INTERPRETATION

What do your dreams reveal about your destiny in God? Find out through a dream interpretation session with Prophet Jeremy Lopez. Contact the offices of Identity Network International today to gain valuable prophetic insight into the world of dreams.

Made in the USA
Columbia, SC
09 September 2023

22623521R10124